Scottish Quakers

and

Early America

1650–1700

by

David Dobson

CLEARFIELD

Printed for
Clearfield Company, Inc. by
Genealogical Publishing Co., Inc.
Baltimore, Maryland
1998

Reprinted for
Clearfield Company, Inc. by
Genealogical Publishing Co., Inc.
Baltimore, Maryland
2000, 2006

International Standard Book Number: 0-8063-4765-1

Made in the United States of America

Table of Contents

Introduction iv

Listing of Scottish Quakers 1

References: Archives and Publications 31

Illustration of a woodblock showing Quakers emigrating 33

Letter from a Scots Quaker in New Jersey, 1684 34

Illustration of the cover of a book about East New Jersey 37

Map of Perth Amboy, about 1700 38-39

Illustration of a print of Aberdeen, Scotland, 1695 40-41

Account of the emigrant ship "Exchange," August, 1683 42

Illustration of a contemporary ship 48

Advertisement to all Trades-men, Husbandmen, Servants
    and others who are willing to transport themselves unto
    the Province of East New Jersey in America 49

INTRODUCTION

Quakerism came to Scotland with the Cromwellian Army of Occupation of the 1650s. The Army was duly purged of Friends in 1657, and some of these men acted as early missionaries in Scotland. These were supported by missionaries based in the north of England, notably the efforts of George Fox during the late 1650s. Scottish Quakers were never numerous and were concentrated in particular locations in Scotland. In the north east the meeting houses were established in Aberdeen, in Kinmuck, and in Ury; in the south east the meeting houses were in Edinburgh and Kelso; in the west of Scotland the meeting house was near Hamilton. Probably the most influential Scots Quakers of the period were George Keith, David Barclay, and Robert Barclay. A feature of late seventeenth-century Scotland was the antagonism between the Episcopal and Presbyterian branches of the Church of Scotland with the virtual persecution of one by the other. Members of the Society of Friends were subject to harassment by both groups and by the civic authorities during much of the period. The persecution that they had suffered during the 1660s and 1670s no doubt influenced their decision to emigrate to America. Another motivating feature was that in 1677 Robert Barclay of Urie visited the Netherlands where he is believed to have met William Penn at the home of Arent Sonnman in Rotterdam. Quakers by then were already established in Pennsylvania and in West New Jersey, and an expansion into East New Jersey by Scots Quakers was a logical development. Between 1682 and 1685 several shiploads of emigrants left the ports of Leith, Montrose, and Aberdeen for East New Jersey. The vessels involved in this emigration were the *Exchange of Stockton,* the *Henry and Frances of Newcastle,* the *Thomas and Benjamin of Montrose,* and the *America.* It should be noted that not all these emigrants were Quakers—some were Covenanter prisoners liberated from prison, while the others were both Presbyterians and Episcopalians. These were not the first Scottish Quakers to settle in America; for example, there were some among the early landowners of West New Jersey in 1664. The Trent family was also responsible for shipping cargoes of prisoners and children from Scotland to Barbados in 1663 and to Pennsylvania in the 1690s.

This publication aims to identify members of the Society of Friends in Scotland prior to 1700 and the Scots origins of many of the Quakers who settled in East New Jersey in the 1680s. The book is based on research carried out in Scotland and in America into both manuscript and published sources.

David Dobson

ADAM, ALEXANDER, born ca.1655, indentured servant shipped to East New
 Jersey on the Henry and Francis 1685, settled in Pitcataway 1685, moved
 to Freehold 1694, married Margaret Eube, children Thomas, Alexander,
 Cornelius, Mary, Margaret, James, Ann, William and David, a
 storekeeper. [NJSA.EJD.A226][MNJ][Lan.165][Minutes of Monmouth
 County, 1688-1721, pp153-154]
AIRDES, ANDREW, married Isobel Gordon, 1685. [SRO.SQR.A.0.34]
ALLAN, HECTOR, skipper in Prestonpans then in Leith, imprisoned on the Bass
 Rock 4.4.1678, [RPC/3.V.436]; transferred to Edinburgh Tolbooth
 31.5.1678, [RPC/3.V.46]; fined 2000 merks for disturbing public worship
 in Prestonpans, Aberdeen, and in North Leith 31.3.1678, [RPC/3.V.477];
 transferred from Edinburgh Tolbooth to Leith Tolbooth 15.8.1678,
 [RPC/3.V.501]; master of the Adventure of Leith, trading between the
 Forth and London during 1680s, [SRO.E72.15.21-23; E72.21.1-4];
 married (1) 4.6.1670 Christian Lindores, who died 8.8.1680, buried in the
 Pleasance 9.8.1680, (2) 4.3.1682 to Agnes Simpson, {widow of James
 Brown in Portsburgh} who died in Hamilton 19.3.1693, children Mary
 b.29.11.1682, buried 14.7.1691 in Pleasance, Hector died 8.12.1684,
 buried in Pleasance 9.12.1684, Hector sr. died 1.4.1686, buried in
 Pleasance 3.4.1686, [SRO.SQR.E.11.1/3/4; E.12.46; E.15.323] testament
 confirmed 1687 Commissariat of Edinburgh
ALLAN, JAMES, married Jean Hamilton at Drumbuy 2.4.1668. children
 Rebecca b.20.2.1669, John 6.7.1671, Jean b.3.2.1674, James b.29.1.1678,
 and Isaac b.24.9.1681. [SRO.SQR.W.16.13/14/16/19/24/28]
ALLAN, JOHN, married Margaret Reid, 29.2.1685. [SRO.SQR.W.16.32]
ALLAN, MARGARET, born before 1682, daughter of James Carlisle and
 Margaret Allan in Leith, settled in Elizabethtown, New Jersey, married
 Eliphet Frazie. [SRO.SQR.E.15.336]
ALLARDYCE, CATHERINE, daughter of James Allardice, wife of John
 Fullarton of Kinnaber, Angus, 1669. [SQS92]
ANDERSON, WILLIAM, weaver in Kelso, children Robert b.12.1.1693, Mary
 b.22.1.1694, died 14.2.1695, buried in Kelso, William b.1.4.1696, Isabel
 b.28.4.1699, and Mary b.29.11.1700, [SRO.SQR.K.17.89/119]
ATKIN, JANET, in Linlithgow, died 20.7.1695, buried in the Pleasance
 21.7.1695. [SRO.SQR.E.11.5]
BAIN, JOHN, resident in England, 'travelling in service of truth', died at Urie late
 1690, buried there. [SRO.SQR.U.3.123]
BAIRD, JOHN, born in Aberdeen ca.1655, indentured servant to East New
 Jersey 1683, settled in Monmouth County, married Mary Hall 1684, father
 of John, David, Andrew and Zebulon, died 4.1755. [NJSA.EJD, Liber A]
 [HOT][MNJ][Lan.188] ?

BAKER, ELIZABETH, from Wallyford, East Lothian, married Bartholemew
    Gibson, smith in the Canongate, at Agnes Brown's house in the West Port
    of Edinburgh, 24.9.1681. [SRO.GD49.17.572]
BAKER, ELIZABETH, witness to a marriage in Edinburgh 24.9.1681.
    [SRO.GD49.17.572]
BARCLAY, DAVID, son of Robert Barclay the elder of Ury, died 1671.
    [SRO.SQR.U.3.122]
BARCLAY, Colonel DAVID, of Urie, Kincardineshire, born 1610, Quaker 1666,
    married Katherine, daughter of Robert Gordon of Gordonstoun 1647,
    father of John, David, Lucy, Jean, and Robert, [HBF.III.64]; prisoner in
    Montrose Tolbooth, [RPC.II.282]; fined £216 Scots, 19.6.1673, for
    attending a conventicle on the northside of Upper Kirk Gate, Aberdeen,
    6.5.1673, [RPC/3.IV.61]; 1676, [ACL.VI.xvi];to be released but confined
    to his country house, 3.4.1677, [ACL.VI.44]; died 12.8.1686, buried at
    Ury. [SRO.SQR.U.3.122;A.0.42]
BARCLAY, DAVID, jr., merchant in Aberdeen, from Aberdeen to East New
    Jersey on the Exchange of Stockton, 6.8.1683, [SRO.E72.15.26]
    [NJHS.MS.IV.5]; from Aberdeen to East New Jersey on the America
    8.1685, [HBF.III.97]; died on voyage to New Jersey 1685.
    [SRO.SQR.U.3.122]
BARCLAY, JAMES, in Achorties, married Janet Wilson in Lethenty, 6.11.1681.
    [SRO.SQR.Kk.1.2]
BARCLAY, JOHN, born 1659, marriage witness in Edinburgh 24.9.1681,
    [SRO.GD49.17.572]; emigrated to East New Jersey 1684, a planter with
    500 acres in Plainfield, and Perth Amboy, New Jersey, 7.1685, witness in
    Woodbridge, New Jersey, 1697*, married Catherine ..., father of John,
    died 1731. [HBF.III.97][Insh.264][*SRO.RD4.83.421, warrant 1501a]
    [NJSA.EJD, Liber A, fo.234/287; Liber b, fo.169]
BARCLAY, ROBERT, born 1648 at Gordonstoun, son of Colonel David Barclay
    of Urie, educated in Paris, returned to Scotland 1664, a merchant in
    Aberdeen, admitted as a burgess of Aberdeen 23.5.1670, at a conventicle
    on Northside of Upper Kirkgate, Aberdeen, 6.5.1673, reference 19.6.1673,
    [RPC/3.IV.61/75]; to be liberated from Montrose Tolbooth 1676,
    [RPC/3.IV.1]; imprisoned in Aberdeen Tolbooth 12.3.1676, [ACL.VI.xvi];
    escaped from Aberdeen Tolbooth, to be captured and imprisoned in
    Edinburgh Tolbooth, 2.5.1677, [ACL.VI.51]; prisoner in Aberdeen
    Tolbooth, moved to Banff 13.6.1677, [ACL.VI.44]; in Holland with Fox
    and Penn during 1677, [BFQ.45]; to New Jersey on the Exchange of
    Stockton, master James Peacock, 8.1683, [NJHS.MS.IV.5]; patent
    18.1.1686, [NJSA.EJD, Liber A, fo.287]; sold land in Monmouth County,
    East New Jersey, via his attorney, 14.3.1690. [NJSA.EJD/B175]
    [NJHS.MS.III/18]; died 1690, married Christian Molleson 11.1669,

children David b.8.9.1670 - died 1671 and buried at Urie, Robert b.
25.1.1672, Margaret b.11.10.1673, she died 1685 and was buried at Ury,
Patience b.25.11.1675, Katherine b.26.6.1677, Christian b.15.5.1680,
David b.17.7.1682, Jean b.27.12.1683, John b.10.8.1687; died 3.10.1690.
[SRO.SQR.U.3.20/60/ 122/131; A.2.45/49/50/52][SQS84-91]

BARCLAY, ROBERT, jr., married Elizabeth, daughter of John Brain a merchant,
in Ratcliff, London 6.6.1696, children Margaret b.23.3.1697, Robert
b.20.6.1699, John b.19.7.1701. [SRO.SQR.A.3.60;U.2.54, 3.20]

BARNES, ROBERT, dyer in Kelso, children Hannah died 1.10.1690, Charles
b.9.2.1693, and Robert b.2.9.1695, son Daniel died in Leith 10.8.1696,
buried in the Pleasance, [SRO.SQR.E.11.3/5; K.17.88/119]; with his wife,
in Leith, 6.3.1696. [South Leith KSR]

BEATTIE, ROBERT, baker in Montrose, married Jean Watson, in Aberdeen
3.5.1683. [SRO.SQR.A.0.30]

BEATTIE, WILLIAM, in Bervie, children Robert b.30.6.1698, and Patience
b.30.5.1702. [SRO.SQR.U.3.60/61]

BIRNIE, ISOBEL, died in Aberdeen 1.11.1688, [SRO.SQR.A.0.49]

BLAIR, THOMAS, missionary in Scotland 1690s. [SQS134]

BLEGBURN, MARGARET, in the Abbey, died 22.1.1681, buried 23.1.1681 in
the Pleasance, [SRO.SQR.E.11.1]

BOIG, WILLIAM, married Isobel Patrick, in Hamilton 30.11.1691.
[SRO.SQR.W.10.86]

BOUSTON, ROBERT, in Darnock, children Joshua b.16.8.1670, Abraham
b.19.7.1671, Elizabeth b.21.1.1673, James b.6.2.1676. [SRO.SQR.K.
17.86/87]

BOWROM, JOHN, born in Yorkshire, missionary in Edinburgh 1653-.[SQS16];
driven from Strathaven, midsummer 1656, and later from Glassford
churchyard 1656. [SQS29]

BOWSTEAD, JOHN, Aglionby, England, attacked in Glasgow and Hamilton
1692. [SQS123]

BRAINE, ALEXANDER, in Woodland, married Christian Sime, 11.8.1696.
[SRO.SQR.Kk.1.32]

BROWN, AGNES, residing at West Port, Edinburgh, 24.9.1681.
[SRO.GD49.17.572]

BROWN, ANDREW, imprisoned in Hamilton Tolbooth, and later in Glasgow
Tolbooth, 1656, [SQS29]; married Jean Hart at Suffield 25.6.1663, she
died 2.1671; he died 25.2.1690, buried at Shawtonhill; children John
b.3.8.1664, Andrew b.20.11.1666, and Thomas b.23.12.1668, died
2.3.1670, [SRO.SQR.W.16.9/10/12/13/15/16/30]

BROWN, ANDREW, in West Mains of Glasford, married Isobel Mitchell,
6.10.1672, children William b.30.7.1674, Marion b. 26.7.1676, Thomas b.
15.11.1678,died 22.3.1681, buried at Shawtonhill, Jean b.16.7.1680, Janet

3

b.24.9.1682, died 11.2.1683, buried at Shawtonhill, Isobel b.8.7.1684,
Elizabeth b.29.1.1686, [SRO.SQR.W.16.17/19/21/24/27/29/30/31/33]

BROWN, JAMES, tanner at the West Port of Edinburgh, to be imprisoned in
Canongate Tolbooth, 4.3.1670, [RPC/3.III.155/162], died 11.1.1681,
buried in the Pleasance 13.1.1681; married Agnes Simpson 5.9.1674,
children Helen b.4.3.1676, [SRO.SQR.E.11.1/2; 12.3/33]

BROWN, JAMES, gardener in Barnton, married Christian Smith 5.8.1682,
children Jean b.8.5.1683, James b.21.5.1685, Mary b.3.8.1686,
[SRO.SQR.E.11.4/5; E.12.47]

BROWN, JOHN, in Deeside, fined £25 Scots by the Privy Council for attending
a conventicle on north side of Kirk Gate, Aberdeen, 6.5.1673,
[RPC/3.IV.61/75]

BROWN, JOHN, in Montquhitter, imprisoned in Aberdeen Tolbooth 12.3.1676,
[ACL.VI.xvi]

BROWN, JOHN, in Raw, parish of Lesmahagow, 11.5.1701, excommunicated
by the Presbytery of Lanark, 12.8.1702. [PL.135-137]

BROWN, JOHN, merchant in Urie, married Julia Smith 7.5.1674, children
Joseph b. 3.3.1675, John b. 20.7.1676, Robert b. 18.1.1678:
[SRO.SQR.A.2.13/49/50/51]

BURGESS, WILLIAM, in Whyterashes, married Margaret Castle, servant to
Margaret Ker, 29.9.1685. [SRO.SQR.Kk.1.9]

BURNESS, JAMES, died 1689, widow Janet Burness in Carntown died 2.1693,
buried at Urie, daughter and son died 1689 [SRO.SQR.U.3.122/123]

BURNETT, ANDREW, indentured servant, from Scotland to East New Jersey
1684, [NJSA.EJD/A] ?

BURNET, ELIZABETH, indentured servant, from Scotland to East New Jersey
11.1684, land grant 1.5.1690, [NJSA.EJD.D167/A197] ?

BURNETT, ROBERT, of Muchalls, 24.6.1669, [RPC/3.III.630]; imprisoned in
Aberdeen Tolbooth 12.3.1676, [ACL.VI.xvi]

BURNETT, Mr ROBERT, son of Sir Alexander Burnett of Leyes, tutor of Leys,
to be brought before the Privy Council 24.6.1669, [RPC/3.III.130];
admitted as a burgess of Aberdeen 9.9.1674, of Lethintie, imprisoned in
Aberdeen Tolbooth 12.3.1676, [ACL.VI.xvi]; prisoner in Aberdeen
Tolbooth, to be released but confined to his country house, 3.4.1677.
[ACL.VI.44]; to East New Jersey on the Exchange of Stockton, master
James Peacock, 8.1683, [NJHS.IV.5]; landowner in ENJ 1683,
[NJSA.EJD.Liber A, fo.88]; Proprietor of East New Jersey, married on
1.12.1682 to Ann ..., father of Patrick, John, Robert, Mesdie, Allan, and
Isabel, settled at Milston Brook, Freehold, Monmouth County, New
Jersey, 1702, probate 16.11.1714 New Jersey, [NJSA.EJD/Liber
1.249/526] [SRO.SQR.E.15.46]

BURNETT, ROBERT, of Cowtoun, Quaker 1680. [Family of Burnett of Leys]

4

BURNETT, WILLIAM, indentured servant, from Scotland to East New Jersey 11.1684. [NJSA.EJD.A197/D197][Insh.242]

BURNYEAT, JOHN, English missionary in Hamilton, Ayrshire and Wigtonshire, 1658. [SQS.25]

BURROUGH, EDWARD, English missionary in Scotland, 1654. [SQS.16]

BUSBY, AGNES, in Kelso, sister of Andrew Busby a wright, died 15.5.1685, [SRO.SQR.K.17.118]

BUSBY, ANDREW, wright in Kelso, married Elizabeth Lamb, {who died 7.1.1688}, children Agnes b.13.7.1685, Agnes b.5.10.1686, died 31.10.1686, Joseph b.25.11.1687, [SRO.SQR.K.17.87/88/118/119]

BUSBY, JANE, in Maxwellhaugh, sister of Andrew Busby wright in Kelso, died 5.12.1672, [SRO.SQR.K.17.118]

BUSBY, or TAILFORD, MARGARET, in Maxwellheugh, mother of Andrew Busby, wright, died 15.4.1681. [SRO.SQR.K.17.118]

CALLENDAR, MICHAEL, gardener at Wallyford, married in Edinburgh on 3.9.1681 to Elizabeth, daughter of Thomas Robertson, gardener in Kelso; later {c.1685}in Langton near Duns, and in West Nisbet {c1691}; children Arent b.9.9.1682, James b. 17.7.1684; Thomas b.7.6.1686, Elizabeth b. 14.4.1688, Michael b.24.2.1690, Sarah b.19.1.1692, Miriam b. 19.1.1692, Abigail b.29.4.1699, Samuel b.2.7.1699, and Elizabeth b.27.7.1703, [SRO.SQR.K.17.87/88/89; E.11.3/4; E.15.333]

CAMPBELL, JAMES, of Nether Stichill, died 30.5.1678, children Catherine died 20.8.1672, John b.4.10.1672, Annabel died 1.1673, Isaac b.25.4.1674, Sarah b. 11.7.1677, [SRO.SQR.K.17.86/87/118]

CAMPBELL, JOHN, settled in Perth Amboy, East New Jersey, 1684.? [Insh.249]

CANT, SARAH, in Aberdeen, 1650s. [VRA]

CAPPIE, ELSPET, in Douglas parish, 6.11.1656, [PL101]

CARLYLE, JAMES, merchant in Edinburgh, married Margaret, daughter of Hector Allen, in Leith 12.2.1681; he died in Aberdeen 20.8.1681, buried there 22.8.1681, daughter Margaret b. 1.4.1682, [SRO.SQR.E.11.3; E.15.331; A.0.24]

CASTELL, MARGARET, died 3.1697. [SRO.SQR.A. 0.120]

CATER, SAMUEL, Isle of Ely, imprisoned in Montrose 1672. [SQS93]

CATON, WILLIAM, born 1636, English missionary in Scotland 1655-. [SQS16]

CATTENACH, GEORGE, a marriage witness in Edinburgh 24.9.1681. [SRO.GD49.17.572]; died 24.7.1695, buried in the Pleasance 27.7.1695. [SRO.SQR.E.11.5]

CHALMERS, JAMES, in Fintray, convicted of holding a meeting in Aberdeen, 2.3.1670. [ACL.V.4]

CHAPMAN, WILLIAM, wright, imprisoned in Aberdeen Tolbooth 12.3.1676, [ACL.VI.xvi]

CHATTO, JANET, married Charles Ormiston, merchant in Kelso, 1651. [OT65]

CHEYNE, CHRISTIAN, indentured servant shipped to East New Jersey by George Keith 2.1685, married Archibald Silver in Matacopine, West New Jersey. [NJSA.EJD.A226.D] ?

CHEYNE, JOHN, indentured as a servant of John Hancock, Horsewynd, the Abbey, Edinburgh, 12.8.1685, for 4 years service in East New Jersey. [NJSA.EJD.A253] ?

CHRISTEN, ROBERT, in Emelton, Northumberland, married Grisel Weir, in Edinburgh, 5.3.1692. [SRO.SQR.E.12.64]

CLARK, WILLIAM, servant to Andrew Jaffray of Kingswells, married Beatrix Thomson, servant to Andrew Somerville, 3.4.1684. [SRO.SQR.A.2.27]; possibly the William Clark who drowned on the voyage to East New Jersey 1684. [Insh.262]

COCKBURN, JOHN, Kelso, settled in Perth-Amboy, East New Jersey, by 1685.? [Insh.277]

COOK, JAMES, married Margaret Brown, in Hamilton 30.5.1669. [SRO.SQR.W.16.114]

CORSTORPHINE, JOHN, in Edinburgh, child Margaret died 17.9.1689, buried in the Pleasance. [SRO.SQR.E.11.4]

COWIE, JOHN, merchant in Aberdeen, fined 100 merks for attending a conventicle on the north side of Kirk Gate, Aberdeen, 6.5.1673, [RPC/3.IV.61/75]; imprisoned in Aberdeen Tolbooth 12.3.1676; escaped from Aberdeen Tolbooth, to be recaptured and imprisoned in Edinburgh Tolbooth, 2.5.1677; prisoner in Aberdeen Tolbooth, to be moved to Banff Tolbooth, 13.6.1677. [ACL.VI.xvi/44/51]

CRAIG, ANDREW, indentured servant, from Scotland to East New Jersey 10.1684. [NJSA.EJD.A266] ?

CRAIG, THOMAS, died 9.3.1691, buried in Strathaven common burial ground 'contrary to his directions'. [SRO.SQR.W.16/28]

CRAWFORD, HEW, gardener in Ormiston, married Isobel Forbes, servant to Bartholemew Gibson, 7.9.1695; daughter Elizabeth b. 1.9.1696, Hew Crawford died 4.5.1704 [SRO.SQR.W.16.40; E.15.344]

CRUICKSHANK, GEORGE, son of John Cruickshank in Balhagartie, married Jean Glenny, 11.6.1697. [SRO.SQR.Kk.1.33]

CUMMING, GEORGE, married Margaret, daughter of James Burness, 1680, settled in Ury, emigrated to New Jersey 1685. [SRO.SQR.U.3.20]

CUTHBERTSON, THOMAS, of Rassriden, child Joshua b. 20.6.1678, [SRO.SQR.K.17.87]

DAVENPORT, ..., Captain Lieutenant of Colonel Daniell's Regiment, in Inverness 3.1657, in Perth 7.1657. [SP.352/362]

DOCKRIE, THOMAS, prisoner in Aberdeen Tolbooth, 5.11.1674, [RPC/3.IV.293]; to be liberated 17.11.1674. [ACL.V.224]

DONALDSON, DAVID, died near Catterline 1689, buried at Urie,
[SRO.SQR.U.3.122]

DUNLOP, THOMAS, weaver in Falkland, married (1)Marion Simpson, children
William 9.11.1677, (2) Margaret daughter of George Fleming in
Linlithgow, 3.12.1680; children George b.17.9.1681, Thomas b.
26.11.1684, b. Bartholemew b.24.12.1686, in Mountholy, Betty b.
20.3.1688, in Grange Loan, Anna b. 20.3.1690, Bartholemew b.
10.6.1692, [SRO.SQR.E.11.2/3/5/6; E.12.3]; his wife and two young
children, ejected from their home in Musselburgh by the magistrates,
appealed to the Privy Council 7.7.1682. [RPC/3.VII.486-7]; in the Grange,
died 26.5.1699, buried in the Pleasance. [SRO.SQR.E.11.6]

EMELTOUN, THOMAS, in Leith, children Charles b.18.5.1670, Elizabeth
b.20.7.1671, Thomas b.17.12.1672 and Samuel b.31.5.1674,
[SRO.SQR.E.11.1; E.12.2]

ELMSLIE, JOHN, in Kilblin, Kinmuck, married Jean Rough, children George b.
17.6.1693, Jean b. 26.2.1695, Mary b. 26.2.1698, John b. 3.11.1702,
Margaret b. 16.6.1704, James b. 14.9.1705, Alexander b. 28.2.1706,
Agnes b. 17.6.1708, John b. 15.9.1709, James b. 21.5.1710, George b.
20.6.1712, Elizabeth b. 29.3.1713, and Alexander b. 20.4.1715,
[SRO.SQR.Kk.1.120]

FALCONER, DAVID, forbidden to conduct marriages, 11.12.1667.
[RPC/3.II.376]; convicted of holding a meeting in Aberdeen 2.3.1670,
[ACL.V.4]; report 1.1.1670 [SRO.CH10.1.65]; bought land in Pleasance,
Edinburgh, 4.1.1674, {a burial ground?}, [SRO.CH10.1.74]; merchant in
Edinburgh 4.1.1676, [SRO.CH10.1.74]; marriage witness in Edinburgh
24.9.1681, [SRO.GD49.17.572]; merchant in Edinburgh, leased 500 acres
in East New Jersey 20.2.1683, similarly 17.6.1690, [NJSA.EJD/A106 :
B/324]; subscribed to the "Account of the Sufferings of the Friends in
Glasgow, 1691" [SRO.CH10.1.65]; married Margaret Molleson 7.3.1672,
{she died in Springhall, Ury, 22.7.1697}; children Margaret b.12.7.1673 -
died 28.2.1676, Christian b.5.7.1674 - died 16.9.1675, John b.11.1.1677,
David b.15.2.1678 - died 20.2.1689, Margaret b. 16.3.1679, Robina b.
15.1.1682 - died 16.5.1683, Robert b.16.12.1683 -died in Mearns 9.1685,
Gilbert b.30.4.1686, and Helen b.14.4.1688, [SRO.SQR.A.0.5/125; E.
11.2/3/4 and 12.3/4,]

FALCONER, DAVID, son of David Falconer in Edinburgh, landowner in Amboy
Point, East New Jersey, 23.11.1682. [NJSA.EJD/A; liber B, fo.324]

FALCONER, JOHN, son of David Falconer in Edinburgh, received land in
Amboy, East New Jersey, 23.11.1682, [NJSA.EJD/A105]; wrote from
London to Friends in Aberdeen 28.2.1709. [SRO.CH10.3.52]

FALCONER, PATRICK, in Elizabeth Town, East New Jersey, 1684. [Insh.245]

FALCONER, PETER, merchant in Woodbridge, East New Jersey, 26.5.1688.

appointed attorney for Alexander Learmonth of Newark; granted letters of administration 1690. [NJSA,EJD, liber B174/420]?

FALCONER, ROBERT, sievewright in Linlithgow, {who died 4.7.1686}, married Elspet, daughter of John Smilly, gardener in West Garshore, 7.3.1674, [SRO.SQR.E.11.4; E.15.325]

FALLOW, JANET {or Agnes?}, wife of John Watson, in Over Stitchill, 3.10.1684. [RPC/3.IX.680]

FEA, RICHARD, prisoner in Edinburgh Tolbooth, 12.3.1665. [ETR]

FELL, CHRISTOPHER, English missionary in Scotland, 1654-. [SQS.16]; in Perth 2.1657, [SP.350]

FERGUSON, GEORGE, son of William Ferguson in Badifarrow, married Elizabeth, daughter of James Gray in Hillocks, 29.3.1692. [SRO.SQR.Kk.1.22]

FERGUSON, GEORGE, married Elizabeth Follow in Bourtrie, 12.6.1694. [SRO.SQR.Kk.1.26]

FERINDALE, OCHILTREE, glover, fined £25 Scots by the Privy Council for attending a conventicle on north side of Kirk Gate, Aberdeen, 6.5.1673, [RPC/3.IV.61/75]; glover, imprisoned in Aberdeen Tolbooth 12.3.1676, [ACL.VI.xvi]; died 17.7.1684. [SRO.SQR.A.0.51]

FINLAY, JAMES, in Garshore, died 2.1680. [SRO.SQR.W.16.27]

FISHER, ANDREW, chapman, imprisoned in Aberdeen Tolbooth 12.3.1676, [ACL.VI.xvi]; a marriage witness in Edinburgh 24.9.1681. [SRO.GD49.17.572]; tanner in West Port of Edinburgh, married Anna Thompson, 15.5.1680, children James b.8.3.1681- died 15.5.1691, Helen b. 5.1.1683 - died 1684, Samuel b.8.2.1685, died 20.10.1694; Andrew Fisher tanner in Portsburgh died 3.12.1687. [SRO.SQR.E.11.1/3/4/6; 12/40]

FORBES, ALEXANDER, of Auchinhamper, Aberdeen, imprisoned in Aberdeen Tolbooth 12.3.1676, [ACL.VI.xvi]

FORBES, ALEXANDER, the elder of Aquhorties, imprisoned in Aberdeen Tolbooth 12.3.1676, [ACL.VI.xvi]; husband of Anne Seaton, [VRA.253]; he died 3.9.1682, she died 4.2.1692. [SRO.SQR.0.22/125]

FORBES, ALEXANDER, second son of Alexander Forbes of Auchorties, apprentice to John Skene, merchant in Aberdeen 31.10.1673, [ARA]; imprisoned in Aberdeen Tolbooth 12.3.1676, [ACL.VI.xvi/xvii]; a marriage witness in Edinburgh 24.9.1681. [SRO.GD49.17.572]; a glover in Edinburgh, died there 21.3.1685. [SRO.SQR.E.11.3]

FORBES, ARTHUR, merchant, from Aberdeen to East New Jersey on the Exchange of Stockton, 8.1683.? [SRO.E72.1.10]

FORBES, GEORGE, merchant in Aberdeen, son of Alexander Forbes in Achorties, married Margaret, daughter of Alexander Skene in Dyce, 26.9.1696. [SRO.SQR.A.2.55]

FORBES, JAMES, convicted of holding a meeting in Aberdeen, 2.3.1670.
[ACL.V.4]

FORBES, Captain JAMES, fined £25 Scots by the Privy Council for attending a
conventicle at the north side of Kirk Gate, Aberdeen, 6.5.1673,
[RPC/3.IV.61/75]; in Bervie, imprisoned in Aberdeen Tolbooth 12.3.
1676, [ACL.VI.xvi]

FORBES, JEAN, daughter of Alexander Forbes, died in Achorties 10.8.1675.
[SRO.SQR.Kk.0.18]

FORBES, JOHN, "a poor boy", prisoner in Aberdeen Tolbooth, 12.1668.
[ACL.IV.282]

FORBES, JOHN, in Auchorties, fined £25 Scots by the Privy Council for
attending a conventicle on north side of Kirk Gate, Aberdeen, 6.5.1673.
[RPC/3.IV.61/75]

FORBES, JOHN, at the Cruives, convicted of holding a meeting in Aberdeen,
2.3.1670. [ACL.V.4]

FORBES, JOHN, in Corse, Aberdeen, fined £25 Scots for attending a conventicle
on north side of Kirk Gate, Aberdeen, 6.5.1673, [RPC/3.IV.61/75];
imprisoned in Aberdeen Tolbooth 12.3.1676, [ACL.VI.xvi]

FORBES, JOHN, eldest son of Alexander Forbes in Achinhamper, married
Barbara Skene, 6.10.1670. [SRO.SQR.A.2.15]

FORBES, JOHN, in Bervie, died 3.9.1682. [SRO.SQR.A.0.26]

FORBES, JOHN, brother of the Laird of Baynlie, landowner in East New Jersey
1684. [NJSA.EJD.Liber A, fo.249]; possibly the brother of the Laird of
Barnla who emigrated from Aberdeen to East New Jersey 1684. [Insh.263]

FORBES, WILLIAM, indentured servant to ENJ 1684. [NJSA. EJD, Liber A]

FORSYTH, MARGARET, died 29.8.1694, buried in Aberdeen
1.9.1694.[SRO.SQR.AM.2.]

FREAR, ..., a hatter from Berwick, son of Robert Frear, died in the Abbey of
Edinburgh 8.9.1700. [SRO.SQR.E.11.7]

FULLARTON, JOHN, of Kinnaber, by Montrose, and his wife Catherine
Allardyce, 1669. [SQS92]

FULLARTON, JOHN, in Kinnaber by Montrose, married Elizabeth Burnett,
widow of Robert Douglas of Tillieghillie, Mearns, in Edinburgh 2.11.1671.
[SRO.SQR.E.12.30]

FULLARTON, ROBERT, Kinnaber, from Montrose to East New Jersey in the
Thomas and Benjamin 1684, settled in Perth Amboy?
[Insh.262][SRO.E72.16.3]

GALBREATH, JOHN, Edinburgh, indentured as a servant to John Hancock for
four years in East New Jersey 12.8.1685. [NJSA.EJD/A252] ?

GALLOWAY, ANDREW, merchant in Aberdeen, fined 100 merks by the Privy
Council for attending a conventicle on north side of Kirk Gate, Aberdeen,
6.5.1673, [RPC/3.IV.61/75]; imprisoned in Aberdeen Tolbooth 12.3.1676;

released 16.5.1677 and re-arrested 14.6.1677, [ACL.VI.xvi/53]; married
(1) Isobel Cushine{?}, children Andrew b.7.2.1672, Patrick b.28.11.1674,
Margaret b.4.1676, (2) Elspet Taylor, children Deborah b.6.1.1681, Anna
b.17.6.1687, Rachel b. 14.4.1689, [SRO.SQR.A.2.45/49/50/51/52/53];
landowner in East New Jersey 1683, [NJSA.EJD, Liber A, fo.85]; died
18.10.1691. [SRO.SQR.A.0.71]

GELLIE, ALEXANDER, of Logie {in 1655}, of Auquhorties {in 1670}, of
Logie Durno {in 1672}, and of Blackfriars {Blackford?}1676, imprisoned
in Aberdeen Tolbooth 12.3.1676, [ACL.VI.xvi]; fined £105 Scots by the
Privy Council for attending a conventicle on the north side of Kirk Gate,
Aberdeen, 6.5.1673, [RPC/3.IV.61/75]; prisoner in Aberdeen Tolbooth, to
be released but confined to his country house, 3.4.1677. [ACL.VI.44];
married (1) Margaret Keillo, who died in Blackfoord 26.3.1674, children
Elizabeth b.5 10 1664, Rachel b. 28.10.1672, (2) Margaret Gordon
22.11.1675, children John b.28.10.1670 in Blackford, Helen b.
18.12.1681, William b. 5.4.1683, Andrew b. 29.5.1684 in Rothway,
Margaret b. 31.3.1688 in Aberdeen, James b.1.2.1694, Sophia b.
28.10.1695 in Blackford, Alexander b. 19.9.1698;
[SRO.SQR.A.2.14/ 44/45/49/50/51/53/54; Kk.1.116/152]

GELLIE, WILLIAM, {MA, King's College, Aberdeen, 1655} in New Milne,
convicted of holding a meeting in Aberdeen 2.3.1670. [ACL.V.4]; fined
£85 Scots by the Privy Council for attending a conventicle on north side of
Kirk Gate, Aberdeen, 6.5.1673; prisoner in Aberdeen Tolbooth 5.11.1674,
[RPC/3.IV.61/75/293]; prisoner in Aberdeen Tolbooth, to be liberated
17.11.1674. [ACL.V.224]; fined for burying his child outwith the town
graveyard 1677, [Aberdeen Gildry Accounts]

GERARD, ROBERT, merchant in Broad Gate, Aberdeen, married Isobel Cowie,
children Margaret died 2.4.1681, Isobel died 8.8.1681, John b. 4.10.1682 -
died 19.4.1694, Anna b. 20.11.1702 {?}, [SRO.SQR.A.0.22/71:
A.2.51/48]; imprisoned in Edinburgh 19.3.1676; released from prison in
Aberdeen 17.5.1677, [ACL.VI.14/54]; he died in Hamburg 16.4.1683.
[SRO.SQR.A.0.30]

GIBSON, BARCLAY, witness to a marriage in Edinburgh, 24.9.1681.
[SRO.GD49.17.572]

GIBSON, BARTHOLEMEW, born 1627, smith in the Canongate, married
Elizabeth Baker from Wallyford, East Lothian, at the house of Agnes
Brown, West Port, Edinburgh, 24.9.1681, [SRO.GD49.17.572]
[SRO.SQR.E.12.45]; H.M. Forger in Edinburgh, leased 10 acres at Amboy
Point, East New Jersey, 23.11.1682. [NJSA.EJD/A112]

GIBSON, JACOB, a marriage witness in Edinburgh 24.9.1681.
[SRO.GD49.17.572]

GIBSON, WILLIAM, a Scottish missionary in Holland [BFQ45] ?

GILFILLAN, JOHN, witness to a deed of factory in Woodbridge, New Jersey, 8.10.1697. [SRO.RD4.83.421, warrant 1501a] Quaker?

GILL, JOHN, a Cumberland missionary, driven from Glassford churchyard 1656. [SQS29]

GLENNIE, ALEXANDER, in Ardoe, convicted of holding a meeting in Aberdeen, 2.3.1670. [ACL.V.4], son died 16.8.1675. [SRO.SQR.A.0.18]

GLENNIE, JOHN, in Colliehill, imprisoned in Aberdeen Tolbooth 12.3.1676, [ACL.VI.xvi]

GLENNY, JOHN, in Mains of Lethenty, son of William Glennie, married Violet Steven, 2.12.1682. [SRO.SQR.Kk.1.6]

GLENNY, JOHN, married Barbara, daughter of Alexander Been in Woodland, parish of Udny, 22.12.1693. [SRO.SQR.Kk.16.36]

GLENNY, WILLIAM, married Margaret Clark, servant to Jean Craig, 21.3.1689. [SRO.SQR.A.2.41]

GOODALL, ANDREW, born 1600, a merchant in Aberdeen, died 1.1674, his widow Elspet Smith died 21.12.1691.. [SRO.SQR.A.0.15/31]

GORDON, ..., and Janet Law, in Maxwellheugh, daughter Elizabeth died 10.9.1667. [SRO.SQR.K.11.8]

GORDON, AUGUSTINE, apothecary in St Buttolph, London, son of Robert Gordon of Cluny deceased, 1690. [NJSA.EJD/B361/362]?

GORDON, CHARLES, son of Robert Gordon of Pitlurg and Catherine Burnett, settled in East New Jersey by 1.1685, died in Perth Amboy, New Jersey, 1698. [NJSA.EJD/A248] ; married Lydia Hampton, children Charles and Peter.

GORDON, GEORGE, of Gordon's Milne, fined £25 Scots by the Privy Council for attending a conventicle on north side of Kirk Gate, Aberdeen, 6.5.1673, [RPC/3.IV.61/75]; probate 20.1.1686 [NJSA.EJD, Liber A, fo.260]

GORDON, GEORGE, merchant, from Leith to East New Jersey on the America, 8.1685. ? [SRO.E72.15.32]

GORDON, GEORGE, planter in East New Jersey, land owner in Perth Amboy ca.1685. [NJSA.EJD.A248]

GORDON, JOHN, in Aberdeen, eldest son of Robert Gordon, died 27.11.1693. [SRO.SQR.A.0.62]

GORDON, ROBERT, married Christian Davidson, children Elizabeth b.25.11.1666, William b.8.3.1668, John b.5.2.1670, Daniel b.29.2.1672, Daniel b.14.4.1675, Gilbert b.7.8.1677, and Isabel b.25.11.1688. [SRO.SQR.A.2.44]

GORDON, ROBERT, in Spittal, imprisoned in Aberdeen Tolbooth 12.3.1676, [ACL.VI.xvi], son died 15.8.1675. [SRO.SQR.A.0.18]

GORDON, ROBERT, in New Place, finded £25 Scots for attending a conventicle on north side of Kirk Gate, Aberdeen, 6.5.1673, [RPC/3.IV.61/75]

GORDON, ROBERT, of Cluny, to New Jersey on the Exchange of Stockton, master James Peacock, 8.1683, [NJHS.MS.IV.5]; landowner in ENJ 1683, [NJSA.EJD, Liber A, fo.86]

GORDON, ROBERT, cardmaker in Aberdeen, landowner in ENJ 1683. [NJSA.EJD, Liber A, fo.88]; cardmaker and widower in Aberdeen, married Elspet Glenny 7.8.1694, daughter Elizabeth b.12.6.1695. [SRO.SQR.A.0.78; 2/44]

GORDON, THOMAS, gentleman in Perth Amboy, East New Jersey, 1686. [NJSA.EJD, Liber A, fo.248]

GORDON, ..., of Lunan, Quaker 1656. [SQS92]

GRAVE, JOHN, missionary in Scotland 1650s. [SQS22-23]

GRAY, ANDREW, in Badcow, married 1688. [SRO.SQR.E.5.49]

GRAY, GEORGE, in New Place, imprisoned in Aberdeen Tolbooth 12.3.1676, [ACL.VI.xvi]; his wife Elspet Webster died 2.2.1679. [SRO.SQR.Kk.1.152]

GRAY, GEORGE, weaver in Hillocks, married Helen Wilson in Aberdeen, 23.8.1681. [SRO.SQR.Kk.1.3]

GRAY, GEORGE, weaver in Aqhorties,died 8.12.1689. [SRO.SQR.A.0.53]

GRAY, JAMES, married Janet Hamilton, widow of Alexander Hamilton of Drumbuy, at Hamilton 26.8.1683. [SRO.SQR.WSM.16.30/EM.15.147]

GRAY, ROBERT, son of Andrew Gray, married Marion, daughter of Robert Gray. 168. [SRO.SQR.E.15.167]

GRAY, WILLIAM, married Anna Findlator, servant to Isobel Cowie a merchant in Aberdeen, 9.12.1688. [SRO.SQR.0.46]

GRAY, WILLIAM, son of George Gray, married Margaret Taylor 27.1.1695. [SRO.SQR.Kk.1.29]

GRAY, WILLIAM, married Janet Martin, 1689. [SRO.SQR.WSM.16.36]

GRIEVE, JOHN, in Pinnacle, children Mary b. 2.5.1672, James b.25.8.1674, and Jane b. 9.1675, [SRO.SQR.K.17/86, 87]

HAIG, ANDREW, in Bemersyde, children David b. 19.12.1669, Hannah b.20.12.1678, [SRO.SQR.K.17/86,87]

HAIG, ANDREW, in Netherstanes, died 25.2.1694, his widow Margaret Dods died 9.1699 [SRO.SQR.K.17.119]

HAIG, ANTHONY, of Bemersyde, born 1639 in Groningen son of David Haig and Hibernia Scholes; Quaker 1657, prisoner in Duns Tolbooth 24.2.1663, transferred to Edinburgh Tolbooth, warded there 17.11.1664, [ETR]; ref. 11.1665; in prison 12.1666; to be released from Edinburgh Tolbooth and allowed to go to Holland to sort out his business matters there, and return within 6 weeks, 8.2.1666, [RPC/3.II.105/135/139]; died 1712.

HAIG, OBADIAH, in New York, 1700. [SRO.RD2.82.739; RD4.85.1]

HAIG, WILLIAM, of Bemersyde, born 28.3.1646 in Berwickshire, son of David Haig of Bemersyde and Hibernia Scholes, a merchant in London, bought land in West New Jersey 1664, married Mary, daughter of Gavin Lawrie, 1673, to America 1683; Receiver General, in Elizabethtown 1685, [NJSA.EJD, liber A, fo.430]; children Obadiah, Lawrie and Rebekah, died in Burlington, New Jersey, 1688. [NYGBR.XXX][NJSA.EJD, Liber A] [HB][SRO.RD2.82.418]

HALHEAD, MILES, English missionary in Galloway 1654-. [SQS16/26]

HALL, JOHN, born in Yorkshire, a missionary in Aberdeen 1658. [SQS26]

HALL, JOHN, merchant in Glasgow, married Elizabeth, eldest daughter of Alexander Gellie in Blackfoord, 5.1.1685 in Aberdeen. children Elizabeth b.17.9.1685, John b.22.6.1687, Margaret b.29.7.1688, Patience b. 10.2.1691, Alexander b.3.5.1692, Benjamin b. 9.2.1694, Agnes b.8.9.1695; he died 15.10.1696. [SRO.SQR.A.0.33/116:A.2.29/52/53/54];

HALLIDAY, ..., prisoner in Aberdeen Tolbooth, to be moved to Banff Tolbooth 13.6.1677. [ACL.VI.44]

HALLIDAY, JAMES, died 20.11.1675. [SRO.SQR.E.11.7]

HALLIDAY, JAMES, the younger, a marriage witness in Edinburgh, 24.9.1681. [SRO.GD49.17.572]

HAMILTON, ALEXANDER, farm worker in Drumboy, near East Kilbride, 1653. [SQS.13]

HAMILTON, ANDREW, portioner of Shawtonhill, died 18.12.1676. [SRO.SQR.W.16.22]

HAMILTON, ANDREW, tailor in Wallyford, married Margaret, daughter of Thomas Cumine in Prestonpans, 7.4.1683. [SRO.SQR.E.15.1340]

HAMILTON, DANIEL, gardener, married Elizabeth Williamson in Aberdeen 21.9.1678, children Jean b.20.1.1680 in Lethenty, Christian died in Grangepans 1686. [SRO.SQR.A.2.18;Kk.1/116; E.11.4]

HAMILTON, HENDRY, in parish of Stitchill, 3.10.1684. [RPC/3.IX.680]; wife Janet Mason died 12.1694 in Stichill; Henry Hamilton in Nether Stichill died 18.1.1702, and Marion Hamilton in Nether Stichill died 18.1.1703. [SRO.SQR.K.17.119]

HAMILTON, or Weir, KATHERINE, in Lesmahagow parish, 6.11.1656, [PL101]

HAMILTON, JAMES, chamberlain of Kinneil, married Elizabeth Williamson who died 10.3.1692, father of Christian who died in Grangepans 18.7.1686. [SRO.SQR.E.11.4/5]

HAMILTON, JOHN, married Margaret Stewart at Drumbuy 29.9.1682, she died 2.1703. [SRO.SQR.W.16.29]

HAMILTON, MARGARET, in Breadyhill, died in the Canongate 22.3.1696. [SRO.SQR.E.11.5]

HAMILTON, MARIAN, in Nether Stitchill, parish of Stitchill, 3.10.1684. [RPC/3.IX.681]

HAMILTON, ROBERT, farmer, Shawtonhill,1679. [SQS121]

13

HAMPTON, ANDREW, tailor in Wallyford, married Margaret Cumine at
Andrew Fisher's house in the West Port of Edinburgh 7.4.1683.
[SRO.SQR.E.12.48; E.15.340]

HAMPTON, JANET, born ca.1668, daughter of John Hampton, indentured
servant shipped to East New Jersey 1684, married Robert Rhea in
Shrewsbury, East New Jersey, 10.2.1690. [NJSA.EJD/A183][MNJ]

HAMPTON, JOHN, gardener in Elphinstone, East Lothian, from Leith to East
New Jersey, arrived at Staten Island 19.3.1683, settled in Perth Amboy
23.11.1683, later in Freehold, married (1) Katherine Cloudsley, at
Alexander Hamilton's house in Drumbuy 7.12.1675; children Elizabeth
b.11.10.1676, Lydia b. 14.5.1678, John b.6.9.1681, [SRO.SQR.W.16.20;
E.11.2];(2) Martha Brown, daughter of Abraham Brown, (3) Jane Curtis or
Osborne, father also of Jane, David, Joseph, Noah, and Jean, died 1.1703.
pro. 26.2.1702, [NJSA.EJD, liberA256/280/434]

HAMPTON, JOHN, son of John Hampton, married Martha, daughter of
Abraham Brown in Shrewsbury, East New Jersey, 3.1.1687. [NJSA]

HANCOCK, FRANCES, widow of Arent Sonmans in Rotterdam, 1696.
[SRO.RD4.78.501]

HANCOCK, JOHN, Edinburgh, a marriage witness in Edinburgh 24.9.1681,
[SRO.GD49.17.572]; from Leith to East New Jersey 1684, died at sea,
[NJSA.EJD/A234]

HARDY, ALEXANDER, indentured servant shipped to East New Jersey by
Gavin Lawrie, 1684. [NJSA.EJD/A] ?

HARDIE, ARCHIBALD, tailor in Lanark, 3.5.1666, [PL106]

HARPER, ALEXANDER, of Easter Echt, fined 200 merks by the Privy Council
for attending a conventicle on the north side of Kirk Gate, Aberdeen,
6.5.1673, [RPC/3.IV.61/75]; imprisoned in Aberdeen Tolbooth 12.3.1676,
[ACL.VI.xvi]

HART, JOHN, farm worker in Heads, parish of Glassford, Lanarkshire,
imprisoned in Hamilton Tolbooth and later in Glasgow Tolbooth 1656,
[SQS.13/29]; married Barbara Hamilton at Shawtonhill 13.7.1665,
[SRO.SQR.WSM.16.11]; in Newton, parish of Avondale, Lanarkshire,
1683. [RPC/3.VIII.652]; children Janet b.7.6.1666- died 5.8.1685, John
b.15.4.1670-died 7.4.1686, wife died 21.1.1693.
[SRO.SQR.W.16.12/15/32/33/37]

HART, WILLIAM, married Jean Brown at Hamilton 8.7.1665,child William
b.5.1666, he died in West Mains of Glassford 26.3.1702.
[SRO.SQR.WSM.16.11/12];

HASTIE, ARCHIBALD, tailor in Lanark, 3.5.1666. [PL.107]

HENEDIE, JOHN, of Cumerheid, parish of Lesmahagow, 1683.
[RPC/3.VIII.658]

HERVIE, JAMES, married Elizabeth Robertson, children Mary b.12.9.1690 in
    Lethenty, John b.26.9.1694, Anna b.20.7.1701, Andrew b. 24.4.1703,
    Elizabeth b. 27.3.1706, Josiah b.5.11.1709, Robert b.15.3.1712,
    [SRO.SQR.Kk.1.116/117]
HOLLAND, GABRIEL, indentured servant shipped to East New Jersey by Gavin
    Lawrie, 1684. [NJSA.EJD/B159] ?
HOPE, ARCHIBALD, son of Henry Hope in the Netherlands, to Pennsylvania
    ca.1677, deed dated 8.6.1683, [Pennsylvania Historical Society MS]
    [BFQ251]
HOPE, HENRY, Scottish merchant in Amsterdam and in Rotterdam, Quaker
    1676. [BFQ.247]
HOPKIRK, JONATHAN, a marriage witness in Edinburgh 24.9.1681.
    [SRO.GD49.17.572]; merchant in Edinburgh, married Elspet, daughter of
    late William Lindores a mercer, at Andrew Fisher's house in the West Port
    of Edinburgh 17.11.1683, children William b.2.12.1686, died 28.7.1695
    [SRO.SQR.E.11.5; E.12.50/15.341];
HUNTER, JOHN, in Fetteresso, in court in Aberdeen 2.3.1670. [ACL.V.4]
HUNTER, JOHN, servant to Robert Barclay of Urie, married Margaret Burnett at
    Urie 1.4.1703. [SRO.SQR.U.3.20]
HUTCHISON, JOHN, shoemaker in Hamilton, married (1) Janet Hamilton
    14.4.1660.{imprisoned in Hamilton on account of their marriage}; (2)
    Janet Mitchell 21.5.1670, children John b.4.9.1671 - died 4.1685, Marion
    b. 4.1.1674, he died 24.3.1686. [SRO.SQR.WSM. 16.6/15/16/20/32/33]
INGLIS, MARY, in Douglas parish, 6.11.1656, [PL101]
ISMAY, RICHARD, imprisoned in Glassford Castle and later in Hamilton
    Tolbooth 1657, [SQS30]
JAFFRAY, ALEXANDER, in Kingswells died 7.5.1673, his widow Sarah Cant
    died 24.8.1673, daughter Sarah died in Edinburgh 14.12.1680.
    [SRO.SQR.A.0.11.14; E.11.1]
JAFFRAY, ALEXANDER, married Christian, daughter of Robert Barclay the
    elder of Ury, 23.2.1700. [SRO.SQR.U.3.20]
JAFFRAY, ANDREW, son of Alexander Jaffray of Kingswells, former Provost
    of Aberdeen, to be brought before the Privy Council, 30.7.1667.
    [RPC/3.II.313]; a prisoner in Banff Tolbooth, to be released on health
    grounds, 3.8.1669, [RPC/3.III.68/640]; married Christian Skene
    13.9.1673, [SRO.SQR.A.0.14]; imprisoned in Aberdeen Tolbooth
    12.3.1676, [ACL.VI.xvi]; prisoner in Aberdeen Tolbooth, to be released
    but confined to his country house, 3.4.1677, [ACL.VI.44]; landowner in
    East New Jersey 1683. [NJSA.EJD, Liber A, fo.83]; youngest son Daniel
    died 24.2.1691, eldest child Lilias born 1674 died 1.4.1694.
    [SRO.SQR.A.0.63/70]
JAFFRAY, MARGARET, Kingswells, 1699. [Aberdeen Presbytery Records.IV]

JOHNSON, ISABEL, servant of Andrew Jaffray, died 24.12.1690.
[SRO.SQR.A.0.63]

JOHNSTON or SKENE, ANNA, in Dyce, died 15.11.1688. [SRO.SQR.A.0.49]

JOHNSTON, WILLIAM doctor of physics, his widow Barbara Forbes died in
Baillieston 19.11.1673. [SRO.SQR.A.0.14]

KEIR, GEORGE, gardener in Colinton, married Isobel Boig in Edinburgh,
24.4.1680, she died 15.8.1699 [SRO.SQR.E.15.329:E.11.7]

KEITH, GEORGE, born in Aberdeen 1638; educated at Marischal College,
Aberdeen; Quaker 1664; to be brought before the Privy Council 30.7.1667.
[RPC/3.II.313]; to be brought before the Privy Council 24.6.1669,
[RPC/3.III.130]; prisoner in Edinburgh Tolbooth 29.7.1669, [ETR]; fined
£25 Scots by the Privy Council for attending a conventicle on north side of
Kirk Gate, Aberdeen, 6.5.1673, [RPC/3.IV.61/75]; portioner of
Bedlesoun, imprisoned in Aberdeen Tolbooth, 12.3.1676, [ACL.VI.xvi];
Mr George Keith of Baylieston, escaped from Aberdeen Tolbooth, later
recaptured and imprisoned in Edinburgh Tolbooth, 2.5.1677, [ACL.VI.51];
prisoner in Aberdeen Tolbooth, moved to Banff Tolbooth 13.6.1677,
[ACL.VI.44]; in Holland 1677, [BFQ.45]; Quaker schoolmaster in London
1682; to East New Jersey with his wife Anna, and daughters Anna and
Elizabeth 2.1685, [NJSA.EJD/A236]; Surveyor General of East New
Jersey; moved to Philadelphia 1689; sold land by Raritan River, 11.6.1690,
[NJSA.EJD/B321]; converted to Episcopalianism in 1700, died in Sussex,
England, 1716. [SQS80]

KEITH, GEORGE, apprentice to John Skene in Aberdeen, imprisoned in
Aberdeen Tolbooth 12.3.1676, [ACL.VI.xvi]

KEITH, GILBERT, weaver, imprisoned in Aberdeen Tolbooth 12.3.1676,
[ACL.VI.xvi]

KEITH, ISABEL, indentured servant, from Scotland to East New Jersey 1684.
[NJSA.EJD.A] ?

KENNEDY, JOHN, in Bankhead, died 2.6.1705. [SRO.SQR.W.16.49]

KER, JAMES, tailor in Dodsland, near Kelso, husband of Margaret Dods who
died 10.11.1694, and father of John who died 15.3.1696, Isabel
b.17.6.1699, and of Jane b.19.12.1703, who died 1.4.1705.
[SRO.SQR.K.17.119/120]

KING, JOHN, in Kinaldie, imprisoned in Aberdeen Tolbooth 12.3.1676,
[ACL.Vi.xvi]; indentured servant, to East New Jersey 1684,
[NJSA.EJD/A]

LACOCKE, JOHN, imprisoned in Hamilton Tolbooth and later in Glasgow
Tolbooth, 1656. [SQS29]

LAING, GEORGE, eldest son of John Laing, formerly of Craigforthie, now in
New Jersey, married Anna, daughter of George Taylor of Kinmuck,
29.8.1688. [SRO.SQR.Kk.11.20]

LAMB, EUPHAN, in Quainscairn, parish of Stitchill, 3.10.1684. [RPC/3.IX.681]
LAMB, ELIZABETH, wife of Andrew Busby wright in Kelso, died 7.1.1688.
[SRO.SQR.K.17.119]
LAMB, ..., wife Christian Grieve who died in Stichill 6.10.1683, son James.
[SRO.SQR.K.17.118]
LAMB, JAMES, and his wife Margaret Busby, in parish of Stichill, 3.10.1684.
[RPC/3.IX.680]; he died in Nether Stichill 15.1.1701, she died
23.10.1704, son Samuel b.2.3.1688. [SRO.SQR.K.17.88/119/120]
LAMB, JANET, in Maxwellheugh, died 21.1.1675. [SRO.SQR.K.17.118]
LANCASTER, JAMES, English missionary in Galloway 1654. [SQS.26]
LAWRIE, GAVIN, emigrated to East New Jersey 1684, Governor of East New
Jersey, husband of Mary ....., father of James, Mary, and Rebecca, patent
for 1000 acres at Cheesequake Bay 28.5.1685, died 1687.
[NJSA.EJD/A183, 190, 240][pro.9.1697 PCC][SRO.RD2.82.418]
LAWRIE, JAMES, son of Gavin Lawrie governor of East New Jersey, 1699.
[SRO.RD2.82.418]
LAWRIE, THOMAS, husband of Elizabeth Wight in Lassudden who died
13.8.1685, father of John b.27.6.1674, Mary b.26.6.1676, Elizabeth
b.13.10.1678 who died 31.11.1687, Christian b.14.7.1681 who died in
Lassudden 10.2.1683, and Thomas b.2.7.1683, Thomas sr. died 21.5.1696.
[SRO.SQR.K.17.118/119]
LAWRIE, THOMAS, brother of Gavin Lawrie, a tailor, emigrated to America
1683, settled at Cheesequake Creek, and later in Freehold, New Jersey,
husband of Rebecca Forrester, father of James and Anna, died 1712.
[MNJ][SRO.RD2.82.418]
LEASK, GEORGE, merchant in Broad Gate, Aberdeen, imprisoned in Leith
19.3.1676, [ACL.VI.14]
LEASK, JAMES, merchant in Aberdeen, escaped from Aberdeen Tolbooth, to be
caught and imprisoned in Edinburgh Tolbooth, 2.5.1677, [ACL.VI.51];
married Isobel Gray, children John died 22.8.1675., Alexander
b.15.6.1682, Margaret and Elizabeth [SRO.SQR.A.10.18; A.2/51/52]
LEASK, JOHN, prisoner in Aberdeen Tolbooth, to be moved to Banff Tolbooth,
13.6.1677. [ACL.VI.44]
LIDDELL, JOHN, weaver in Hamilton, married Margaret Burden widow of
Thomas Biers late cordiner at the Water of Leith, in Edinburgh 2.11.1700,
son Isaac b.3.6.1702. [SRO.SQR.E.12/81]
LIDDELL, JOHN, weaver in Colinton, husband of Margaret ... who died
22.11.1705, father of John who died 19.12.1706. [SRO.SQR.E.11.7;
W.16.40]
LINDORES, CHRISTIAN, wife of Hector Allan skipper in Leith, died 8.8.1680,
buried in the Pleasance 9.8.1680. [SRO.SQR.E.11/1]

17

LIVINGSTONE, PATRICK, report 1.1.1670, [SRO.CH10.1.65]; prisoner in Aberdeen Tolbooth, to be moved to Banff Tolbooth, 13.6.1677. [ACL.VI.44]; marriage witness in Edinburgh 24.9.1681, [SRO.GD49.17.572]; children stillborn 1.9.1686; Patrick b.25.9.1687, Patrick sr. died 15.4.1694. [SRO.SQR.A.0.42; Kk.17.119]

LOW, WILLIAM, weaver, in Cotton of Kinnaber, married Katherine, daughter of Alexander Steel a cordiner in Fetteresso, 27.9.1673, [SRO.SQR.A.0.14]; prisoner in Montrose Tolbooth, to be liberated 1676, [RPC/3.IV.1]

MCKENZIE, JOHN, prisoner in Edinburgh Tolbooth, 12.3.1665. [ETR]

MARTIN, ALEXANDER, married Isobel Liddell, 1681. [SRO.SQR.W.16.28]

MARTIN, WILLIAM, married Margaret Smaily, 14.8.1671, she died in Strongate 2.10.1692, daughters Margaret b.16.7.1672 and Mary b.9.12.1677. [SRO.SQR.W.16.16/17/37]

MASON, JANET, wife of Hendry Hamilton, in Stitchill parish, 3.10.1684. [RPC/3.IX.680]

MEARNS, WILLIAM, smith in Newplace, married Margaret Tindall, servant in Aberdeen, 13.4.1694. [SRO.SQR.A.0.71]

MELVIN, GEORGE, in Ury, died 11.2.1698, his wife died 2.1698. [SRO.SQR.U.3.123]

MELVIN, JAMES, married Elspet Sharp, 1677. [SRO.SQR.U.3.20]

MERCER, JOHN, sr., widower in Pitmuckston, married Anna, daughter of John King a dyer in Aberdeen, in Aberdeen 17.2.1701. [SRO.SQR.A.4/5]

MERCER, THOMAS, merchant and late Dean of Guild in Aberdeen, fined 100 merks by the Privy Council for attending a conventicle on north side of Kirk Gate, Aberdeen, 6.5.1673, [RPC/3.IV.61/75]; married Margaret Gregorie, sons Joseph who died 4.5.1673, and John b.8.1674, [SRO.SQR.A.0.11]; a leading Quaker imprisoned in Aberdeen Tolbooth 12.3.1676; escaped from Aberdeen Tolbooth, to be recaptured and imprisoned in Edinburgh Tolbooth, 2.5.1677; prisoner in Aberdeen Tolbooth, to be moved to Banff Tolbooth, 13.6.1677; to be released from Aberdeen Tolbooth, 16.2.1678, [ACL.VI.xvi/44/51/101]; he died 16.2.1697. [SRO.SQR.A.0.118]

MIDDLETON, ALEXANDER, married Agnes Burgess in Aberdeen 8.4.1695. [SRO.SQR.A.2.63]

MILL, ALEXANDER, servant to Thomas Mercer, salmonfisher, died 2.4.1692. [SRO.SQR.A.0.31]

MILL, JEAN, daughter of Alexander Mill, in Bridge of Dee, died 5.1681. [SRO.SQR.A.0.23]

MILL, JOHN, son of Alexander Mill in Kingswells, married Janet, daughter of James Taylor in Inverurie, 8.11.1683. [SRO.SQR.A.2.52]

MILLER, JAMES, married Margaret Robertson, 12.1690, she died 9.8.1691. [SRO.SQR.W.16.36]

MILLER, JOHN, married Katherine Hamilton 25.6.1682.
[SRO.SQR.WSM.16.29]
MILLER, WILLIAM, gardener, married Margaret Cassie, in Hamilton
27.6.1680, daughter who died in New Port Glasgow 1.3.1681 and buried
at Kilmacolm, children George b.2.2.1682, William b.23.3.1684, Isaac
b.7.7.1686, Joseph b.7.7.1686 died in Partick 1.1688 and buried at
Garshore, Hew b. 7.11.1689 at the Abbey of Edinburgh, Margaret
b.22.2.1692, died at the Abbey of Edinburgh 22.2.1692, Margaret born
7.5.1693 died 19.9.1700; Elizabeth b.20.9.1695, Joseph b.27.12.1698,
wife Margaret died in the Abbey of Edinburgh 13.5.1702.
[SRO.SQR.A.0.20; E.11.6/7]
MILNE, JOHN, in Fintray, imprisoned in Aberdeen Tolbooth 12.3.1676,
[ACL.VI.xvi]
MILNE, JOHN, weaver, prisoner in Montrose Tolbooth 8.2.1672,
[RPC/3.III.605]; weaver in Cotton of Kinnaber, married Margaret Walker,
servant to William Napier, in Kinnaber by Montrose 13.4.1674,
[SRO.SQR.A.0.16]; to be liberated 1676, [RPC/3.IV.1]
MILNE, THOMAS, shoemaker in Aberdeen, married Jean Innes or Stenhouse,
father of Priscilla b.17.4.1672, [SRO.SQR.A.2.45]; buried a child in the
Quaker Yard, Gallowgate, Aberdeen, c.1672, [Extr. Abdn. Burgh
Rec.p280]; fined £25 Scots for attending a conventicle on north side of
Kirk Gate, Aberdeen, 6.5.1673, [RPC.IV.61/75]; imprisoned in Aberdeen
Tolbooth 12.3.1676; prisoner in Aberdeen Tolbooth, to be moved to Banff
Tolbooth 13.6.1677. [ACL.VI.xvi/44]; children died 1671 and 3.1672;
widow died 11.7.1684. [SRO.SQR.A.0.13/32]
MITCHELL, ANDREW, married Janet Weir, 22.9.1677 at Southfield, she died
22.2.1704, daughter Mary b.20.2.1679. [SRO.SQR.W.16.23/25]
MITCHELL, JANET, in Douglas parish, 6.11.1656, [PL101]; died 7.1.1689.
[SRO.SQR.W.16.36]
MITCHELL, JOHN, in Douglas parish, 6.11.1656, [PL101]; died 19.4.1668.
[SRO.SQR.W.16.3]
MITCHELL, MARION, in Douglas parish, 6.11.1656, [PL101]
MITCHELL, MARY, widow, with four sons, shipped to East New Jersey by
Arent Sonmans, petitioned the Governor 29.2.1683. [NJSA.EJD] ?
MITCHELL, WILLIAM, in Douglas town, parish of Douglas, Lanarkshire,
6.11.1656, [PL.101]; married Mary Inglis in Douglas 10.1656,
[SRO.SQR.W.16.1];1683. [RPC/3.VIII.657]; died 2.12.1687,
[SRO.SQR.W.16.34]
MOLLISON, GILBERT, merchant and baillie of Aberdeen, married Margaret ...,
children Gilbert (burgess of Aberdeen 7.5.1660), John (burgess of
Aberdeen 26.9.1676), Christian b.18.7.1647 (married Robert Barclay at
Echt). [SRO.SQR.U.3.27]

MOLLISON, GILBERT, wrote from London to Friends in Aberdeen, 28.2.1709 and 15.6.1709.[SRO.CH10.3.52]

MOLLISON, JAMES, married Elspet, daughter of George Johnston, at Tillakeirie 4.4.1674, [SRO.SQR.A.0.16]

MONRO, DANIEL, in London, married Margaret, daughter of John Ker in New Machar, 2.1.1687. [SRO.SQR.A.0.43]

MONTGOMERIE, WILLIAM, born ca.1655, eldest son of Hew Montgomerie of Bridgend, married Isobel, daughter of Robert Burnet of Lethentie 1684, emigrated to America 1701, settled at Doctor's Creek, East New Jersey. [History of the County of Ayr ?

MOORE, ANDREW, tanner in Edinburgh, married (1) Janet Adamson from Midlothian, 4.4.1672; (2) Elizabeth Cumine, 27.11.1677; Andrew Moor in Waughton, died 3.3.1695; widow Elizabeth died 9.1.1701 in St Germans, East Lothian, children Benjamin b.3.4.1674 at Prestonhaugh, Elizabeth b.18.9.1678 at Prestonhaugh, Margaret b.10.3.1685 at Waughton, Nathaniel b.15.9.1687, Alexander b.7.12.1690, and George b.16.1.1692. [SRO.SQR.E.11.5/7; E.15.324/326]

MORRISON, JOHN, tobacco merchant in Hamilton, son of Duncan Morrison a tobacco merchant, married Helen, daughter of Andrew White in Lesmahagow, 26.4.1690, children John b.26.3.1699 and Margaret b.19.6.1701. [SRO.SQR.W.16.42]

MORRISON, JOHN, son of William Morrison and Jean Cunningham in Castle Drummond, Perthshire, married Grissell, daughter of Andrew and Christian Whyte in Douglas, 30.10.1698. [SRO.SQR.W.14.7]

MUIR, ALEXANDER, son of Alexander Muir, hookmaker in Aberdeen, fined £25 Scots by the Privy Council for attending a conventicle on north side of Kirk Gate, Aberdeen, 6.5.1673, [RPC/3.IV.61/75]; in Aberdeen, 1676, [ACL.VI.xvi]; married Margaret, in Tulliekerrie, {died 29.4.1681} daughter of George Chalmer, husbandman in Fintray, 5.10.1673, father of Edward died 6.4.1681. [SRO.SQR.A.0.14/22]

NAPIER, ALEXANDER, indentured servant shipped to East New Jersey 1684. [NJSA.EJD/A183] ; due headland 22.1.1690. [NJSA.EJD/B133]

NAPIER, WILLIAM, shipmaster and merchant in Montrose, prisoner in Montrose Tolbooth 18.2.1672, [RPC/3.III.441-448, 605][SQS93]; to be liberated from Montrose Tolbooth, 1676, [RPC/3.IV.1, 668-670]; master of the Hope of Montrose, 1663, ["Aberdeen Shore Works Accounts, 1596-1670" p.497]; married (1) Marie, daughter of Harry Hope in Rotterdam, at Patrick Livingstone's house in Edinburgh 2.3.1683; married (2) Sibella, eldest daughter of Robert Falconer in Tayock 19.11.1670, [SRO.SQR.A.2.7; E.15.339]; master of Marie of Montrose 1684 [SRO.E72.16.12]

NAYLOR, JAMES, Englishman, Quartermaster of Lambert's Horse in the Parliamentary Army which invaded Scotland, at Dunbar 1650, Quaker 1651. [SQS15]

NEILL, JOHN, a marriage witness in Edinburgh 24.9.1681,[SRO.GD49.17.572]; a tailor and freeman of Potterrow, Edinburgh, married Mary, daughter of James Halliday, at Andrew Fisher's house in the West Port of Edinburgh 31.11.1682; parents of James b.12.9.1683 - died 8.12.1684, Helen b.3.2.1682 - died 20.4.1687, Agnes b.27.11.1687 - died 27.11.1687. [SRO.SQR.E.11.3/4; E.15.338]

NEILL, WILLIAM, tanner in Portsburgh, a marriage witness in Edinburgh 24.9.1681; married Isobel Milne 2.4.1681, parents of Helen b.3.2.1682, Margaret b.12.2.1684, and Agnes b.21.8.1686; he died 27.11.1687 [SRO.GD41.17.572][SRO.SQR.E.11.1/3/4/5; E.15.332]

NEILL, ..., in Glasgow, 1691. [SQS134]

NICOLL, JAMES, in Montrose, prisoner in Montrose Tolbooth, 18.2.1672, [RPC/3.III.605]; to be liberated from Montrose Tolbooth, 1676, [RPC/3.III.1]; married Agnes, sister of John Fullarton of Kinnaber, at Cotton of Kinnaber 4.6.1678. [SRO.SQR.A.2.16]

OLIPHANT, JOHN, husband of Janet Gilchrist, father of Margaret and Janet, in Pencaitland, East Lothian, indentured as servants to John Hancock in Edinburgh 19.8.1685. [NJSA.EJD/A252] ?

ORMISTON, CHARLES, born 1625, merchant in Kelso, Quaker 1665, married Janet Chatto 1651, father of John b.6.1662, Charles b.1.4.1667, and Joseph b.6.3.1669, [SRO.SQR.K.17.86], died 21.12.1684, [OT65]; to be arrested and imprisoned in Edinburgh Tolbooth 1.2.1666; to be released from Edinburgh Tolbooth 20.2.1668; prisoner in Canongate Tolbooth 4.3.1670; to be freed from Edinburgh Tolbooth 7.4.1670; prisoner in Kelso Tolbooth, 1673. [RPC/3.II.135/411; III.155/162; IV.33], he died 19.12.1684. [SRO.SQR.K.17.118]

ORMISTON, CHARLES, jr., born 1667, merchant in Kelso, father of Richard b.5.9.1694 - died 7.1.1705, Jane b.17.2.1696, Elizabeth b.17.8.1697, Margaret b.11.9.1698 - died 19.9.1698, and John b.25.1.1700 - died 11.2.1700, Mary b.24.5.1701 - died 3.8.1704, Rachel died 20.8.1704. [SRO.SQR.K.17.88/89/119/120]

OSBORNE, WILLIAM, Scottish, Lieutenant Colonel of the Parliamentary Army, resident in Edinburgh, to Badcow 1656. [SQS.18]

PARKER, ALEXANDER, English missionary in Scotlamd 1657. [SQS34]

PATERSON, ALEXANDER, in Aberdeen, 1675, [ACL.VI.xvii]

PATTERSON, JOHN, shoemaker in Carlisle, married Janet, daughter of Robert Stratton an apothecary in Dundee, 12.10.1678. [SRO.SQR.E.12.38]

PHALP, MARGARET, died 29.7.1676. [SRO.SQR.W.16.21]

PHILSHER, ANDREW, widower and a cooper in Gorbals, Glasgow, married Margaret, second daughter of George Gray in Achorties, 6.12.1700 in Edinburgh. [SRO.SQR.E.12.80;15.108]

PORTER, JAMES, widower in Tillieberrie, married Elizabeth Blackhall in Brunthill, 15.2.1685. [SRO.SQR.Kk.1.10]

PURDEN, JOHN, in Partick, married Margaret Simpson in Erskine, 28.10.1685; a widower, married Janet Neil, 1698. [SRO.SQR.W.14.8; W.16.35]

PURDIE, JAMES, married Helen Reid, in Edinburgh 19.9.1693. [SRO.SQR.E.12.66]

RAE, RICHARD, shoemaker, prisoner in Aberdeen Tolbooth, resident in Edinburgh 1670-1675. [SQS.13]; cordiner in the West Port of Edinburgh, died 4.3.1681. [SRO.SQR.E.11.1]

RAEBURN,................., merchant in Kelso, to be arrested and imprisoner in Edinburgh Tolbooth, 1.2.1666. [RPC/3.II.135]

RAMSAY, EUPHANE, prisoner in Edinburgh Tolbooth, 12.3.1665, [ETR]

REDFORD, ANDREW, in Midlem, died 4.8.1685, father of Joseph b.20.5.1675, and Benjamin b.10.3.1678. [SRO.SQR.K.17.87/118]

REDFORD, THOMAS, father of Samuel b.22.5.1674. [SRO.SQR.K.17.86]

REDFORD, THOMAS, indentured servant, shipped to East New Jersey 1684. [NJSA.EJD/A][Lan.188]

REDFORD, WILLIAM, born in Friershaw, Teviotdale, 1642, indentured servant of Arent Sonmans, shipped to East New Jersey 1682, land grant in Essex County, East New Jersey, 1692, died 1.3.1725. [NJSA/EJD/A114/D]

REDFORD, WILLIAM, in Barlands, father of Samuel b.6.8.1675, Andrew b.31.8.1676, Margaret b.21.1.1678, and William b.23.1.1678. [SRO.SQR.K.17.87]

REID, ANDREW, son of John Reid, emigrated to East New Jersey on the Exchange 1683, died 1769. [MNJ]

REID, ALEXANDER, married Katherine Reith, parnets of John b.27.8.1696, Daniel b.1.3.1699, and William b.11.7.1700. [SRO.SQR.Kk.1.116/118]

REID, ANDREW, subscribed to certificate, Edinburgh 9.8.1792 [SRO.CH10.]

REID, GEORGE, indentured servant, shipped to East New Jersey 1684. [NJSA.EJD/A]

REID, JAMES, married Jean Hamilton, ca.1680. [SRO.SQR.WSM.16.27]

REID, JAMES, son of John Reid, to East New Jersey on the Exchange 1683, settled in Perth Amboy and later in Freehold, Monmouth County, died ca.1711. [MNJ]; sold land in Monmouth County 1690, [NJSA.EJD/B326]

REID, JOHN, born 16.2.1656, gardener, married Margaret Miller 29.11.1678, parents of Anna b.24.11.1679, Helen b.2.8.1681, and Margaret b.11.3.1683, bookseller in Edinburgh, author of 'The Scotch Gardener', leader of emigrants on the Exchange, Captain James Peacock, from Leith and Aberdeen to East New Jersey 8.1683, arrived at Staten Island

19.12.1683, settled in Perth Amboy and later in Hortencie, Monmouth
County, died 16.11.1723. [MNJ][NJHS:MS.III/18][NJSA.EJD, Liber A,
fo.438/439][SRO.SQR.E.11.3; W.16.24]
REID, MARJORY, prisoner in Edinburgh Tolbooth, 12.3.1665, [ETR]
RHEA, ROBERT, carpenter, emigrated to East New Jersey 1685, settled in
Monmouth County 1688, married Janet Hampton in Shrewsbury
10.2.1690, he died 18.1.1720, she died 15.1.1761.
[MNJ][NJSA.EJD,Liber B164]
RITCHIE, ALEXANDER, indentured as a servant in Edinburgh to John Hancock
for 4 years in East New Jersey 12.8.1685. [NJSA.EJD.A252] ?
ROBERTSON, ESTER, daughter of Thomas Robertson in Bridgend, Kelso,
married 2.9.1699. [SRO.SQR.E.15.96]
ROBERTSON, JOHN, of Ethie in Ross, imprisoned in Aberdeen Tolbooth
12.3.1676, [ACL.VI.xvi]
ROBERTSON, JOHN, married Christian Chalmers, father of Elizabeth
b.10.10.1672. [SRO.SQR.Kk.1.116]; possibly the Quaker schoolmaster at
Kinmuck 1681-17... [SQS110]
ROBERTSON, ROBERT, married Isobel, daughter of Robert Gordon a merchant
in Aberdeen, 5.7.1700. [SRO.SQR.A.4.3]
ROBERTSON, THOMAS, missionary in Scotland 1657. [SQS26]
ROBERTSON, THOMAS, gardener at Bridgend of Kelso, married Margaret
Hanna, father of Thomas died 2.8.1670, Esther b.20.3.1672, Samuel
b.22.5.1674, Thomas died 30.9.1698, Margaret died 23.2.1683.
[SRO.SQR.K.17.86/118/119]
ROBERTSON, WILLIAM, physician in Burntisland, married Margaret Allen,
{widow of James Carlyle} 5.8.1682 in Edinburgh, parents of William
b.17.5.1683, and Elizabeth b.24.2.1685, emigrated to East New Jersey,
settled in Monmouth County 19.7.1690.
[NJSA.EJD/D209][SRO.SQR.E.11.4/15.336]
ROBISON, ANDREW, prisoner in Duns Tolbooth 24.2.1663, transferred to
Edinburgh Tolbooth 7.3.1663, warded there 7.3.1663, [ETR]; ref.
11.1665; in prison 12.1666, [RPC/3.II.105/135]; temporarily released from
Edinburgh Tolbooth, 12.2.1668 to 15.3.1668, [ETR]
ROBINSON, MARGARET, indentured servant, shipped to East New Jersey by
Gavin Lawrie 1684. [NJSA.EJD/A] ?
ROBINSON, PATRICK, in Linlithgow, 1688. [SQS123]
ROSS, ALEXANDER, born 1682, shipped to Philadelphia by Maurice Trent,
indentured for 10 years in Chester County, Pennsylvania, 3.10.1693, a
Quaker convert. [SG.29/1.11]
ROSS, JAMES, married Anna Kerson in Old Bourtrie, 12.4.1693 in Kinmuck.
[SRO.SQR.Kk.1.30]

ROYLE, MARY, shipped to Philadelphia by Maurice Trent, indentured for 5
    years in Chester County, Pennsylvania, 14.7.1697, [SG.29/1.11]
RUSSELL, CHRISTIAN, in Angus 1656. [SQS92]
SANDILAND, JAMES, a soldier, arrived in Pennsylvania 1668, father of Mary
    Sandilands, died 1692, {Quaker?} [SG.29/1/11]
SANDILANDS, ROBERT, {3rd son of Mr James Sandilands, town clerk of
    Aberdeen} prisoner in Aberdeen Tolbooth, to be liberated 11.11.1676,
    {later a clergyman of the Church of England} [ACL.V.37; VI.xvii]
SCOTT, GIDEON, of Highchester. [SQS102]
SCOTT, JAMES, married Christian Boag servant of David Falconer in Kirkhill,
    at Montrose 24.3.1691. [SRO.SQR.A.2/43]
SCOTT, JOHN, brewer in Leith, 13.7.1676, [South Leith KSR]; fined 100 rex
    dollars and ordered from Leith 29.8.1676, [RPC/3.V.39]; three children
    buried 1672/1673. {Greyfriars}
SCOTT, ROBERT, born in Montrose 1647, settled in Stonehaven, married Janet
    Keith, 15.4.1680, son John b.1.2.1687. [SRO.SQR.A.2.19; U.3.129]
SCOTT, THOMAS, married Marjory Sloan in Aberdeen 5.5.1672.
    [SRO.SQR.A.0/5]
SCOTT, WALTER, of Raeburn, third son of Walter Scott of Harden and
    Lessuden, and his wife, ref. 22.6.1665, prisoner in Edinburgh Tolbooth
    7.1666, taken to Jedburgh Tolbooth, 2.8.1666; to be imprisoned in
    Jedburgh Tolbooth 24.6.1669; to be freed from the Tolbooth but restricted
    to his home, 1.1.1670; prisoner in Canongate Tolbooth 4.3.1670,
    [RPC/3.II.57/177/187; III.114/130/155]
SCOTT, ..., daughter of William Scott in Old Aberdeen, died 2.10.1675.
    [SRO.SQR.A.0.18]
SCOTT, WILLIAM, merchant in Aberdeen, imprisoned in Aberdeen Tolbooth
    12.3.1676, [ACL.VI.xvi]
SCOTT, ..., son of .... Scott in Stonehaven, dead by 1689. [SRO.SQR.U.3.122]
SCULLER, WILLIAM, a marriage witness in Edinburgh 24.9.1681.
    [SRO.GD49.17.572]
SEATON, ALEXANDER, married Janet Simson, Gorbals, Glasgow, father of
    William b.20.2.1695, and of Alexander b.14.11.1697.
    [SRO.SQR.W.16.39]
SETON, Sir ALEXANDER, imprisoned in Aberdeen Tolbooth 12.3.1676,
    [ACL.VI.xvi]
SHARP, PATRICK, farmer in Kingswells, married Agnes, daughter of James
    Burness cordiner in Ury, 29.6.1678. [SRO.SQR.U.3.20]
SHARP, PETER, in Deeside, died 7.9.1691. [SRO.SQR.A.0.71, 211]
SHAW, JAMES, son of John Shaw and Janet Woodall in Hamilton, died
    2.6.1679. [SRO.SQR.W.16.25]

SHERRILAW, ROBERT, in the parish of Lesmahagow, excommunicated by the Presbytery of Lanark 12.8.1702. [PL.137]

SILVER, ARCHIBALD, married Christian Cheyne in Matacopine, West New Jersey 16.. [NJSA.EJD.A226.D]   ?

SILVER, JAMES, in Fetteresso, convicted of holding a meeting in Aberdeen, 2.3.1670, [ACL.V.4]

SIME, JOHN, married Jean Ferguson, in Lethenty, children Christine b.4.10.1670, Isabel b.1.2.1678, John b.7.5.1680, Jean b.1.8.1682, Margaret b.15.2.1685, and Alexander b.4.1.1691. [SRO.SQR.Kk.1.116]

SIMPSON, AGNES, or Brown, widow of Hector Allan skipper in Leith, moved to Hamilton, died 19.3.1693, buried in the Pleasance 23.3.1693, [SRO.SQR.E.11.3; W.16.37]

SIMPSON, DANIEL, married Helen Corbet, daughter Christian b.29.1.1695. [SRO.SQR.A.2.48/53]

SIMPSON, JANET, in Hamilton, died 21.11.1688. [SRO.SQR.W.16.35]

SIMPSON, WILLIAM, subscribed to the "Annual Report" 1.1.1670, [SRO.CH10.1.65]; married Helen Gilberson, 3.1.1670. [SRO.SQR.W.16.15]

SKENE, Mr ALEXANDER, of Newtyle, son of Robert Skene and Margery Forbes, baillie and magistrate of Aberdeen, married Lilias Gillespie 1646, father of John, [VRA.242]; imprisoned in Aberdeen Tolbooth 12.3. 1676, [ACL.VI.xvi]; prisoner in Aberdeen Tolbooth, to be released but confined to his country house, 3.4.1677. [ACL.VI.44]; he died at Kingswells 7.3.1693, she died 21.4.1697. [SRO.SQR.A.0.51/120]

SKENE, JOHN, merchant in Aberdeen, purchased land in West New Jersey 1664, married Helen, daughter of John Fullarton in Kinnaber 23.10.1669, father of Katherine, Lilias b.2.1673, Marie 3.12.1674, and Christine b.6.3.1675 [SRO.SQR.A.2.1; A.2.45/46/47/49]; a leading Quaker imprisoned in Aberdeen Tolbooth 12.3.1676, [ACL.VI.xvi]; reference 19.6.1673, attended a conventicle on northside of Upper Kirk Gate, Aberdeen, 6.5.1673, [RPC/3.IV.61]; escaped from Aberdeen Tolbooth, to be recaptured and imprisoned in Edinburgh Tolbooth, 2.5.1677; prisoner in Aberdeen Tolbooth, to be moved to Banff Tolbooth, 13.6.1677. [ACL.VI.44/51]

SMAILLY, ROBERT, married Agnes Thomson, son Matthew b.21.11.1681 in Garshore. [SRO.SQR.W.16.27]

SMITH, JAMES, indentured servant shipped to East New Jersey by John Forbes 10.1684, [NJSA.EJD/A266]

SMITH, JOHN, married Margaret, daughter of Thomas Cargie in Ury, 8.10.1698, children Margaret b.28.10.1699 and Elizabeth b.17.3.1701. [SRO.SQR.U.3.20/60/61]

SMITH, WILLIAM, married Marie Steven, father of Marie b.4.7.1694.
[SRO.SQR.Kk.1.116]

SOMERVILLE, ALEXANDER, mariner in Aberdeen; convicted of holding a
meeting in Aberdeen 2.3.1670. [ACL.V.4]; married Jean Craig 19.2.1670;
children Samuel b.24.8.1672, possibly died 5.1673, Marie b.3.12.1673 and
John b.16.2.1676, [SRO.SQR.A.0.13; A.2.5/45/50]; imprisoned in
Aberdeen Tolbooth 12.3.1676; as a pilot and mariner to be released from
prison for 24 hours, 3.4.1677, [ACL.VI.xvi/45]; burgess of Aberdeen
1686. [Aberdeen Burgess Register]

SOMERVILLE, JOHN, married Isobel, daughter of James Leask, merchant in
Aberdeen, 23.4.1695. [SRO.SQR.A.2.60]

SONNEMANS, ARENT, in Rotterdam, married (2) Frances White, nee
Hancock, widow of John Swinton; killed by highwaymen in Huntingdon,
England, 4.1683. [BFQ131]; marriage witness in Edinburgh 24.9.1681.
[SRO.GD49.17.572]

SONNEMANS, FRANCES, a marriage witness in Edinburgh 24.9.1681.
[SRO.GD49.17.572]

SONNEMANS, JOHANNA, a marriage witness in Edinburgh, 24.9.1681.
[SRO.GD49.17.572]

SONNEMANS, PETER, son of Arent Sonnemans, in Perth Amboy, executor of
John Hancock 1686, [NJSA.EJD, Liber A, fo.234]; patent 17.2.1686,
[NJSA.EJD, liber A, fo.287]; appointed Miles Forster as his attorney in
East New Jersey 14.5.1688, [NJSA.EJD liberB143]; merchant in London
1689, [NJSA.EJD/B143]; educated at Leiden University, emigrated to East
New Jersey 1705. [BFQ.131]

SONNEMANS, RACHEL, a marriage witness in Edinburgh 24.9.1681.
[SRO.GD49.17.572]

SPARK, WILLIAM, in Stonehaven, accused of holding a meeting in Aberdeen,
2.3.1670. [ACL.V.4]; in Dunnottar, 9.10.1672, [SF]; 1676, [ACL.Vi.xvi]

SPEAR, ARCHIBALD, tailor in Prestonpans, married Katherine, daughter of
Francis Wood, a gardener in Duddingston, 7.3.1674, she died in Hamilton
19.1.1679, he died 6.3.1679, son Hew b.3.9.1677. [SRO.SQR.E.15.325;
W.16.25]

STEVEN, ALEXANDER, weaver, father of child died 6.1673.
[SRO.SQR.A.0.13]

STEVEN, ALEXANDER, stabler in Aberdeen, father of George b.11.9.1690,
and William b.9.2.1694. [SRO.SQR.A.2.53]

STEVEN, WILLIAM, weaver in Tarwells, died 11.8.1675, buried at Achorties.
[SRO.SQR.Kk.1.152]

STEVEN, WILLIAM, in Bourtrie, imprisoned in Aberdeen Tolbooth 12.3.1676,
[ACL.VI.xvi]

STEVEN, WILLIAM, died 12.1679, buried at Achorties. [SRO.SQR.Kk.1.152]

STEVENSON, GAVIN, married Grissell Hamilton, 14.10.1659.
[SRO.SQR.WSM.16.5]
STEWART, ALEXANDER, shipped to Philadelphia by Maurice Trent,
indentured in Chester County, Pennsylvania, 5.8.1697 for 8 years, a
Quaker convert. [SG.29.1.11]
STIRLING, ISOBEL, daughter of James Stirling a merchant in Edinburgh, died
19.1.1685. [SRO.SQR.E.11.1]
STIRLING, KATHRINE, died in Edinburgh 2.6.1684. [SRO.SQR.E.11.1]
STOCKDALE, WILLIAM, English missionary, driven from Strathaven,
midsummer 1656, and later from Glassford churchyard 1656. [SQS29]
STORY, CHRISTOPHER, English missionary in Scotland, 1690s.[SQS134]
STORY, THOMAS, Justicetown, near Carlisle, attacked in Glasgow and
Hamilton 1692. [SQS123]
STOT, JAMES, in Old Meldrum, married Helen Castle in Achorties, 27.9.1687.
[SRO.SQE.Kk.1.16]
STOT, WILLIAM, in Old Meldrum, married Margaret Ferguson in Inverurie,
23.8.1687. [SRO.SQR.Kk.1.18]
STRACHAN, JANET, in Musselburgh, died 29.2.1692. [SRO.SQR.E.11.4]
STUBBS, JOHN, English missionary in Scotland 1654-. [SQS16]
SWAN, GEORGE, innkeeper in Edinburgh, settled in Gorbals, Glasgow, about
1687. [SQS135]
SWINTON, ALEXANDER, a marriage witness in Edinburgh 24.9.1681.
[SRO.GD49.17.572]; died in the Abbey of Edinburgh 15.8.1687.
[SRO.SQR.11.4]
SWINTON, JOHN, of Swinton, Quaker 1657, prisoner in Newgate, London,
1660, shipped to Leith, imprisoned in Edinburgh. [SQS98]; married {1}
Margaret Stewart, daughter of Lord Blantyre, {2} Frances Hancock,
widow of ... White, who later married Arent Sonnemans. [OT128]; with
his daughter and son John prisoners in Edinburgh Tolbooth 12.3.1665,
[ETR]; transferred to Edinburgh Castle 7.4.1665, [ETR]; to be imprisoned
in Stirling Castle 24.6.1669; prisoner in Canongate Tolbooth 4.3.1670; to
be released from Montrose Tolbooth 19.12.1672,
[RPC/3.III.130/155/615]; died at Borthwick 1679. [SQS99]
SWINTON, JOHN, merchant in Edinburgh, married Sara ..., son Archibald
b.26.10.1683. [SRO.SQR.E.12/4]
TAYLOR, WILLIAM, married Margaret, daughter of William Gray, a saddler,
burgess of Aberdeen, 19.10.1686. [SRO.SQR.A.0.42]
TAYLOR, WILLIAM, born in England, died 12.1.1698. [SRO.SQR.A.0.128]
TAYLOR, WILLIAM, died 12.12.1706. [SRO.SQR.AM.3]
TAYS, JAMES, in Douglas town, parish of Douglas, Lanarkshire, 1683.
[RPC/3.VIII.657]

THOMSON, JOHN, in West Port of Edinburgh, died 1.11.1695.
[SRO.SQR.E.11.5]

TOD, ROBERT, in Douglas parish, 6.11.1656, [PL101]

TRENT, MAURICE, merchant in Leith, husband of Janet Young cnf 1.12.1669
Edinburgh; landowner in West New Jersey 1664. [NYGBR.XXX]; a
marriage witness in Edinburgh 24.9.1681, [SRO.GD49.17.572]; a mariner
in Philadelphia 1682, [SG.29/1/11]; married Mary Sandilands, daughter of
James Sandilands, [SG.29/1/11]; merchant in Leith, 1694,
[SRO.RD4.75.1128]; died 25.11.1700. [SRO.SQR.E.11.7]

TRENT, WILLIAM, merchant in Inverness, married Mary Burge, father of
Maurice and James, 16... [SG.29/1/11]

TROUP, GEORGE, married Marjorie Ritchie, servant to John Hall a merchant in
Aberdeen, 8.4.1695, children Christine b.6.1696, Elizabeth b.2.11.1697,
David b.31.11.1700 and Robert b.20.9.1703. [SRO.SQR.A.2.62;
U.3.60/61]

URQUHART, JAMES, married Isobel Johnston, 17.8.1680 in Lethenty,
[SRO.SQR.Kk.1.1]

VALENTINE, ROBERT, in Kinmuck, married Christian Porter in Brunthill,
7.4.1685. [SRO.SQR.Kk.1.7]

WALLACE, DAVID, b. in Arbuthnott 1660, married Elizabeth, daughter of
Robert Gordon burgess of Aberdeen, 5.8.1687, she died 24.1.1690;
children Robert b.20.5.1688, died 25.6.1689, David b.8.2.1690, Patience
b.31.6.1698, and Elizabeth b.2.12.1700. [SRO.SQR.A.0.44/51/53; A.2.52;
U.3.60/130]

WALLACE, DAVID, married Margaret Hampton, late servant to Charles
Ormiston merchant in Kelso, at Urie 11.4.1695. [SRO.SQR.A.2.61]

WALLACE, JAMES, married Margaret Taylor, 9.7.1694, she died 16.2.1707.
[SRO.SQR.Kk.1.28; A.0.8]

WATKINSON, Captain GEORGE, Parliamentary officer in Scotland, cashiered
for his beliefs 1657. [SQS42]

WATSON, HELEN, servant to Alexander Hamilton, died 28.7.1676.
[SRO.SQR.W.16.21]

WATSON, JAMES, born 1640, died 8.1.1703. [SRO.SQR.W.16.8]

WATSON, JOHN, in Over Stitchill, 3.10.1684. [RPC/3.IX.681]

WATSON, PETER, possibly from Selkirk, to East New Jersey with David
Barclay as an indentured servant 1683, settled in Perth-Amboy, planter at
Matawan or New Aberdeen, father of Richard. ? [Insh.247]

WEBSTER, WILLIAM, in Hillocks, married Agnes Reid, 15.9.1681.
[SRO.SQR.Kk.1.4]

WEDDERBURN, ABRAHAM, married Isobel Amos, father of Isobel or
Margaret b. 29.8.1677 in Prestonpans. [SRO.SQR.E.11/1]

WEIR, GEORGE, son of Katherine Hamilton, in Lesmahagow parish, 6.11.1656, [PL101]; married Janet Hamilton at Shawtonhill 19.9.1669, parents of Katherine b.8.8.1670, and of John in Southfield who died 10.5.1677. [SRO.SQR.W.10.15; W.16.14/23]

WEIR, KATHERINE, daughter of Katherine Hamilton, in Lesmahagow parish, 6.11.1656, [PL101]

WEIR, JANET, daughter of Katherine Hamilton, in Lesmahagow parish, 6.11.1656, [PL101]

WEIR, JEAN, wife of Andrew Robison, prisoner in Edinburgh Tolbooth, 12.3.1665. [ETR]

WELSH, MARGARET, indentured servant shipped to East New Jersey by James Johnston 10.1685, transferred to Robert Turner in Philadelphia 10.3.1689, then to George Lockhart in New York 21.4.1690 [NJSA.EJD/A226-B158]

WELSH, MARY, daughter of William Welsh in Edinburgh, married John Osgood in London 167... [BFQ220]

WELSH, SARAH, daughter of William Welsh in Edinburgh, married John Swinton jr., from Edinburgh, in London 1674, [BFQ.220]

WELSH, WILLIAM, husband of Sarah ...., Quaker merchant in Edinburgh 1657, moved to Rotterdam by 1661, to London 1663, purchased land in West New Jersey 1664, [NYBGR.XXX]; settled there 1683, moved to Newcastle, Delaware, died there, buried in Chester, Pennsylvania, 1684, father of Sarah and Mary, [BFQ.220]

WHAP, AGNES, died 20.3.1693, Edinburgh. [SRO.SQR.E.11/5]

WHYTLIE, MATTHEW, feltmaker, prisoner in Edinburgh Tolbooth, 12.3.1665, [ETR]; liberated 20.4.1665, [ETR]

WHITLAW, WILLIAM, gardener, married Helen Haddow in Erskine, at Hamilton 8.2.1692, she died 5.8.1701. [SRO.SQR.W.16.37; E.11.7]

WIDDERS, ROBERT, English missionary in Scotland 1657. [SQS34]

WIGHAM, ANTHONY, subscribed to a certificate in Edinburgh 12.12.1816. [SRO.CH10]

WILLIAMSON, JEAN, b.1622, resident of Aberdeen, died 16.11.1714. [SRO.SQR.A.0/60, 2/31]

WILSON, JAMES, workman at the West Port of Edinburgh, married Margaret Rait, father of Anna b.23.11.1685. [SRO.SQR.11.5]

WILSON, ..., in Perth 2.1657. [SP.350]

WINCHESTER, ROBERT, married Margaret Kennedy, servant to Adam Smith a merchant in Aberdeen, 6.5.1686 in Aberdeen. [SRO.SQR.A.2.31]

WISHART, WILLIAM, of New Milne of Crimond, imprisoned in Aberdeen Tolbooth 12.3.1676. [ACL.VI.xvi]

WOOD, ALEXANDER, born 11.11.1669 son of Hew Wood and Agnes Black, died 6.12.1702, married Sarah ....., father of Joseph b.26.11.1697 in Hamilton. [SRO.SQR.W.16.14/40]

WOOD, HEW, gardener to the Duke of Hamilton, subscribed to a report
    1.1.1670, married Grisel Richardson, 6.9.1671, he died 25.3.1701, she
    died 20.4.1705. [SRO.SQR.W.16.16/17; CH10.1.65]
WOOD, JAMES, gardener, son of Hew Wood, gardener in Hamilton, married
    Abigail Robertson, 6.1.1684, she died in Drumlanridge 14.4.1693; father
    of Hew b.28.6.1685, Thomas b. 9.3.1687 in Drumlanridge, James
    b.16.4.1689, Abigail b.5.4.1691 and of Mary born in Fetteresso
    20.12.1697. [SRO.SQR.E.15.342; W.16.17/32/34/36; U.3.60]
WOOD, WILLIAM, married Margaret Anderson, in Triochquaire, father of Anna
    b.24.8.1687. [SRO.SQR.W.16.37]
WRIGHT, BESSY, in Maxwellheugh, d.22.2.1689. [SRO.SQR.K.17.119]
YOUNG, ROBERT, marriage witness in Edinburgh, 24.9.1681.
    [SRO.GD49.17.572]

REFERENCES

ARCHIVES

SRO = Scottish Record Office, Edinburgh
CH=Church Records
E= Exchequer Records
GD=Gifts and Deposits
RD= Register of Deeds
SQR=Scottish Quaker Records,
    A= Aberdeen Meeting
    E= Edinburgh Meeting
    K= Kelso Meeting
    Kk= Kinmuck Meeting
    U= Ury Meeting
    W= West of Scotland Meeting
NJHS = New Jersey Historical Society, Newark
NJSA = New Jersey State Archives, Trenton
EJD=East Jersey Deeds
PRO = Public Record Office, London
PCC= Prerogative Court of Canterbury

PUBLICATIONS

ACL= Aberdeen Council Letters
BFQ= Benjamin Furly and Quakerism in Rotterdam,[W.Hull, Swarthmore,1941]
ETR = Edinburgh Tolbooth Records
HBF = A History of the Barclay Family H F Barclay, [London, 1934]
Insh = Scottish Colonial Schemes 1620-1686, G.P.Insh [Glasgow, 1922]
Lan. = Scotland and Its First American Colony, 1683-1765, N.Landsman,
    [Princeton, 1985]
MNJ = History of Monmouth, New Jersey
NYBGR= New York Genealogical & Biographical Record, series, New York
PL = The Presbytery of Lanark, 1623-1709, [Edinburgh, 1839]
RPC= Register of the Privy Council of Scotland, series, [Edinburgh]
SF = The Synod of Fife, [Edinburgh 1837]
SG = The Scottish Genealogist, series, [Edinburgh]
SP = Scotland and the Protectorate, C H Firth, [Edinburgh, 1899]
SQS = The Story of Quakerism in Scotland,1650-1850,G.Burnet, [London, 1952]
VRA=Valuation Rolls of the County of Aberdeenshire 1667, A&H Taylor,
    [Aberdeen, 1933]

Quakers emigrating

(2) A Double of a Letter from New Perth, date the 1 of the seventh month, 1684, from John Reid, who was Gardener to the Lord Advocate, to a Friend at Edinburgh.

" Seeing it hath pleased God to bring me and mine safe unto this port, I took upon myself as obliged to write something according to my promise of this countrey : indeed I must say its a brave place, but I have not had time to take such observations as I would, being so ingadged to attend my other businesse. Here is no outward want, especially of provisions, and if people were industrious they might have cloaths also within themselves ; by the report of all, its the best of all the neighbouring Collonies, it is very wholesome, pleasant and a fertile land : there are also some barren lands, viz white Sandy land, full of Pine trees, it lyes betwixt South River and Barnegate or Neversink, (albeit there be also much good land in that precinct,) yet its a good place for raising a stock of cattle, providing they have large room to run in, for cattle finds good food there in winter, when none is in the best land, and therefore do the inhabitants provide little hay in winter. The soyl of the country is generally a red marle earth with a surface of black mould (nor doth it appear what really it is to their eyes who cannot penetrate beyond the surface) full freighted with grass, pleasant herbs and

flowers, and in many places little or no wood, but most places full of large timber, as walnut, especially oak ; there be some places here and there in the woods, they call swamps, which is low Ground amidst or betwixt rising ground full of bushes, which holds water in winter, the most of them be dry in Summer, but these being cleared, and some of them that needs being drained, are the richest land. Here are great conveniencies of Bay, Sounds, Rivers, Creeks, Brooks, and Springs, all over the Province, but one of the best things is the large quantities of brave Meadowes, both salt and fresh, which makes the people here able to supply their Neighbours as they doe, throw the abundance of their cattle. I know one Planter who hath a hundred of cattle, not above three years settled ; and no wonder, for some of the grass is as high as my head. Its a pity to see so much good land as

I have been over in this province lying waste, and greater pity to see so much good and convenient land taken and not improven.

As soon as any of the land here comes to be cultivated, it over-runs with small Clover-grass, by the pasturage and dunging of cattle, and so supplants the naturall grass and herbs, notwithstanding of their quick and strong growth. Fruit trees also prosper well here. Newark made about a thousand barrells of Sider last year (a barrel is 8 Scots gallons) this is like that of Woodbridge, who made 500 barrells of pork, in one year, before the law was made against the Swines trespassing.

Here they sow most Indian corn, and wheat ; some Rye, Barly, Oats : Indian corn the first year that they break up or plough, the second they sow Wheat, because the spontaneous growth of the weeds is done away by howing the Indian corn, as we do cabbage : here is one planter makes accompt, That he hath about three thousand bushels of wheat reapt this year : I suppose he hath above a hundred acres of it, but I doe not make these instances as so many precedents.

I know nothing wanting here, except that good Tradesmen, and good Husbandmen, and Labourers are scarce : a Labourer may have a bushell of Corn per day, when he is a little acquainted with the work of the Country, but Tradesmen much more. Smiths, Carpenters, Masons, Weavers, Taylors, Shoemakers, are very acceptable : any who comes let them bring some cloaths and their tools with them, as used in England, and provide butter, bisket, wine, and especially beer and ale, for their Sea voyage, besides the Ships allowance ; and they need not fear when they come here, albeit they have no more, yet they will be better if they have something either in money or Scots linnin and stuffs to buy a little provision at first, to set them up a house and buy a cow or two ; and tho a man be rich, I would not advise him to bring many servants, at least not to keep many at first, untill he see about him and know what he is doing.

I cannot tell what goods are best to bring, David Barclay can tell better ; But he who brings money may expect 15d for the English 5 shil : some may bring a little of the best wheat for a change of seed, and some barly and Oats, for the same use : also a little Scots field peas, there being none such here ; bring also some clover seed.

There are a great store of Garden herbs here, I have not had time to inquire into them all, neither to send some of the many pleasant (tho to me unknown) plants of this Countrey, to James Sutherland, Physick Gardener at Edinburgh, but tell him, I will not forget him, when opportunity offers.

I had forgot to write of Ambo, or New Perth, therefore I add, that it is one of the best places in America, by the report of all Travellers, for a town of trade ; for my part I never saw any so conveniently seated : this with my love, and my wife's to all friends, and acquaintances.

I Rest thy friend

JOHN REID."

THE
MODEL

GOVERNMENT

OF the

PROVINCE

OF

EAST-NEW-JERSEY

IN

AMERICA

And Encouragements for such as Designs
to be concerned there.

Published for Information of such as are de-
sirous to be Interested in that place.

EDINBURGH,

Printed by *John Reid,* Anno
DOM. 1685.

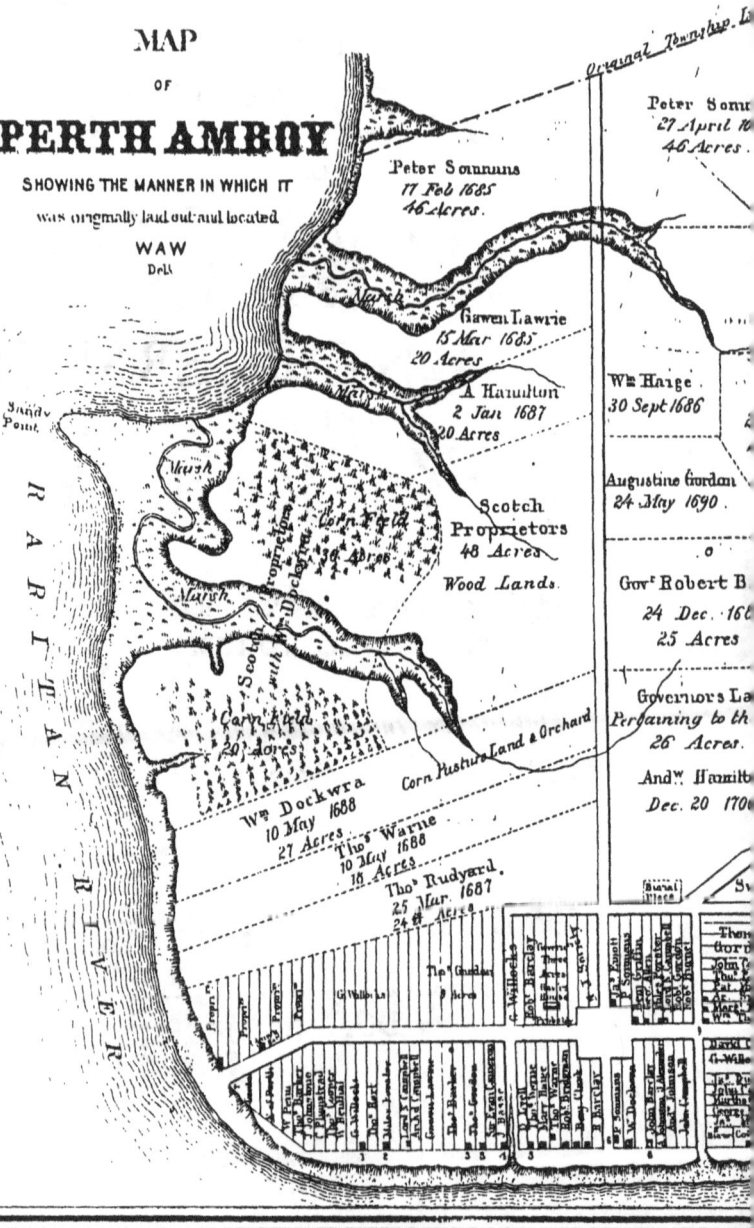

MAP

OF

PERTH AMBOY

SHOWING THE MANNER IN WHICH IT

was originally laid out and located

WAW
Del.

RARITAN RIVER

Sandy
Point.

Peter Sonmans
17 Feb 1685
46 Acres.

Peter Som
27 April 16
46 Acres

North

Gawen Lawrie
15 Mar 1685
20 Acres

W.m Haige
30 Sept 1686

A Hamilton
2 Jan 1687
20 Acres

Augustine Gordon
24 May 1690

Marsh

Scotch Proprietors
Corn Field
16 Acres

Scotch
Proprietors
48 Acres

Wood Lands.

Gov.r Robert B
24 Dec. 16
25 Acres

Marsh

Scotch Proprietors with Dock there

Governors La
Pertaining to th
26 Acres.

Corn Field
20 Acres

Corn Pasture Land & Orchard

And.w Hamilton
Dec. 20 170

W.m Dockwra
10 May 1688
27 Acres

Tho.s Warne
10 May 1688
18 Acres

Tho.s Rudyard.
25 Mar. 1687
24 Acres

Burial
Place

Peter Watson 25 Acres

James Reed 25 Acres

Thomas Gordon
25 Nov. 1699

J. Johnstone
24 May 1690
64 Acres

E. Cameron
24 May 1690
84 Acres

To Piscataway

To Woodbridge

Geo Willocks

17 June 1701.

John Johnstone
6 June 1701

W:m Penn
16 May 1693
25 Acres

Tho: Barker
10 July 1688.
12¼ Acres

Thomas Hart
25 June 1687.
25 Acres

Clement Plumstead
10 May 1688
12¾ Acres

T. Cooper
10 May 1688
12½ Acres

Old Bounds

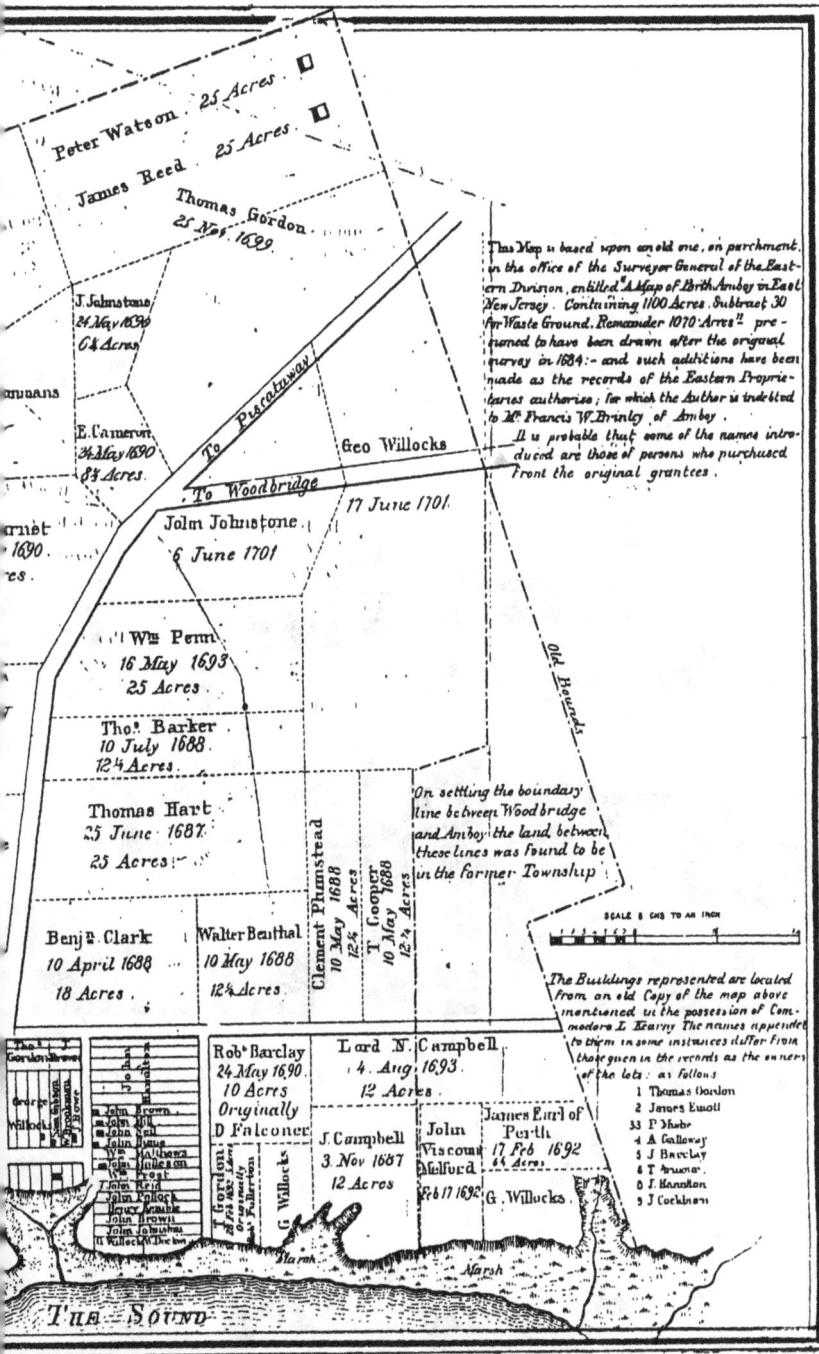

This Map is based upon an old one, on parchment,
in the office of the Surveyor General of the Eastern Division, entitled "A Map of Perth Amboy in East
New Jersey. Containing 1100 Acres. Subtract 30
for Waste Ground. Remainder 1070 Acres" pre-
sumed to have been drawn after the original
survey in 1684:– and such additions have been
made as the records of the Eastern Proprie-
taries authorise; for which the Author is indebted
to Mr Francis W. Brinley of Amboy.
It is probable that some of the names intro-
duced are those of persons who purchased
from the original grantees.

On settling the boundary
line between Woodbridge
and Amboy the land between
these lines was found to be
in the former Township

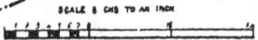

SCALE 8 CHS TO AN INCH

The Buildings represented are located
from an old Copy of the map above
mentioned in the possession of Com-
modore L. Kearny. The names appended
to them in some instances differ from
those given in the records as the owners
of the lots: as follows

1 Thomas Gordon
2 James Emott
33 P. Shobe
4 A Galloway
5 J Barclay
6 T Armour
7 D. J. Hamilton
9 J Cockburn

Benj:a Clark
10 April 1688
18 Acres

Walter Benthal
10 May 1688
12½ Acres

Rob:t Barclay
24 May 1690
10 Acres
Originally
D Falconer

J. Campbell
3. Nov 1687
12 Acres

Lord N. Campbell
4. Aug. 1693.
12 Acres

John
Viscount
Melford

James Earl of
Perth
17 Feb 1692
44 Acres

Feb 17 1692. G. Willocks

John Brown
John Neil
John Jones
W:m Halbana
John Anderson
T Frost
John Reid
John Pollock
Henry Krunkle
John Brown
John Johnston
H Willocks the son

G. Willocks

T Gordon
afterwards J Barclay
Originally D Falconer

Marsh

Marsh

THE SOUND

Facies Ciuitatis ABERDONIÆ Veteris.

The Prospect of Old ABERDIEN.

41

Account of Shipment to East Jersey, in August, 1683, by Some of the Proprietors.

[From a Copy among the Manuscripts of W. A. Whitehead.]

A BREIFF ACCOUNT of the Disposall of the Joynt Stock sent úpon the Shipp Exchange James Peacock M.ʳ the Last of August 1683. By David Barclay To East Jersey, by some of the Proprietors thereof;

Viz.ᵗ There was Caryed over in goods. The Servants, freight, & some of the oat-meal which was sould here again, and all other charges Deducted out of the . . . } £945. ═ ═

Note, the charges of furnishing out the two overseers and all the servants cost above 300℔ only a few beds &c: in-cluded which made in all as above . . . . } £344.18 ═

So that there was in goods but . . . . . £600. 2. ═

In 1684] Memorandum of this. ther is in Catle in the overseers and servants custody Viz.ᵗ

John Hanton hath	.	9 Cowes
John Reid	. . .	8.
James Reid and Peter watson 4.	In all 21 Cowes and 15 Calves	

More. John Hanton received 6 oxen
James Reid and Peter watson 4
John Reid . . . 6 In all 16 oxen

It Makes 37.

A Bull in halve for acco.ᵗ William Dockwra

This is 37 head of Catle, besides the 15 Calves, and a Bull bought in partnershipp with John Carrington overseer to W.ᵐ Dockwra the cost and Charges of them all amounts to . . £155.15.

42

In horses and Mares as follows vizt

John Hanton hath 2 horses and 1 mare

John Reid . 2

—————
4

James Reid and Peter Watson 2 mares

—————
8

Horses & Mares In all 7. cost £38. 9.2½

In Breeding Sowes, vizt

John Hanton receaved 2.

John Reid . . 4.

James Reid and partner 2. In all 8 cost . . . £8. 4.5½

Delivered in provisions vtensills and necessarys to John Hanton the value of £144. 6.11

Delivered to John Reid in provisions & necessaries . . £147. 2.=

Delivered to James Reid and peter watson in provisions and }
necessaries the value of . . . . . . } £30. 2. 6

Disbu·st for several publick charges on the companys acco^t }
and for building John Reid houses as p. account . } £212.10. 1

Quo theise 3 Articles of John Barclay & the overseers	Left in goods and provisions vizt corn and pork in the Cuntry the value of . . . £81.17. 7
	In Debts there the value of . £105.= =
	In John Marsh hands for build- } ing John Hantons house . } £35.10. 9

My expences in the Country & passage to London . . £48. 4 —

Brought over with me having Deducted nothing for my owne }
provision being 20 Months in the companyes service }. £58.18. 4
£47^{lb} 2^s 10¹ starling is in that Country money . . }

¹ So that the Stock in Cattle & ye building & all }
charges in settling cost . . . . . } Totall £1066. 1. 7

And the Servants to remaine for 4 Yeare from their
first tyme

This is David Barclays Abstract of things wherein I am
concerned one hundred pounds stock. a true Coppie of
what he gave to me WILL: DOCKWRA

The large acco^t of particulars are entred in the books

———————————————————

¹ What follows is in the hand-writing of W. Dockwra. Ep.

43

Account of the Respective Interests in the Cargo of the Ship Exchange, Sent to East Jersey, in August, 1683.

[From a Contemporaneous Copy among the Manuscripts of W. A. Whitehead.]

The Cargo Sent over with David Barclay Yonger to East new Jersey belonging to severall Proprietors and others after named concerned in the Said Province in the Ship Called the Exchange of Stockton James Peacock Master which Sailed from Aberdeen the Last of August 1683, being examined according to the particular Invoice of goodes thereof left and Subscribed by David Barclay appears in whole to be 973 : 5 : 9¼

Which as it was at Severall times by parcels in money and goodes delivered to him, standeth as followeth.

	℔ sh d
from Arent Sonmans in goodes } bought by him at Edenbrough }	024:09:03¼
from him in Cash . . .	075:00:00
from him more in Cash, there being included in this 15: he received from Bart: Gibson for a lott in Ambo point . .	107:06:09½
from him in goodes from Holland	158:03:11
from him in Cash . . .	038:02:04½
from him in goodes from Holland	023:05:00
from him in goodes from London	031:00:00

℔: Ss d
457:07:04½

NOTE
they arrived not vntill Mid: }
Decemb. being 3mo & ¾ passage }

It is to be noted that all the Summes placed to A. S. Credit on the other side amounting to 457 : 7 : 4½, there is to be deduced 100 to Perth Lundie and Tarbutt, which they allowed to him in theire accoumpts (viz) 50 to Lundie, 25 to Perth, and 25 to Tarbutt, So rests of A. S 357: 7: 4½, and out of this is to be deduced 15ᵇ he received from Bart. Gibson for a share in Ambo point which lott of 10 Acres someing off proportionably of all the Shares concerned in the Stock being 8¼ Proprieties whereof 3¾ belongs to A. S. viz his owne, that in Bart. Gibsons name, that in Gawen Lawries name, and the halfe in John Hancocks name, the partners one, Robert Gordon and Gawen Lawrie one, William Dockwra one therefore this 15 being divided amongst the 8¼ to the 5 will belong 8 : 17. and to A. S 6. 3. So that the Stock on the other side is thus proportioned the 8℔: 17 being deduced as above there is belonging

	℔: Ss d
To Arent Sonmans children . . .	348:10:04¼
To Perth Lundie and Tarbutt . .	100:00:00

	£ s. d. fr.	£ s. d. fr.
To Robert Barclay		100:00:00
To Robert Burnett and partners		124:16:02
To William Dockwra		100:00:00
To be devided among the last 5. for the reason above mentioned which is to each: 1: 15: 4: 3⅗		008:17:00
To David ffalconer.		050:00:00
To David Barclay		010:10:00
To Ballance given out for Meale by Robert Burnett which being left behind, 1 and Sold repaid him		026:17:03
Also to Ballance to be paid the Master of ffraught in Jersey he wanted		033:05:00
		973:05: 9½

	£ s. d. fr.	£ s. d. fr.
frm Robert Burnett by bill on John Drummond	012:10:00	
from him in Cash	058:06:08	
from him more in Cash	051:13:05	
from him more in Cash	029:03:04	151:13:05
from Robert Barclay		100:00:00
from Robert Gordon of Cluney		050:00:00
from Gawen Lawrie		050:00:00
from William Dockwra		100:00:00
from David ffalconar in goodes		050:00:00
Advanced by David Barclay		010:10:00
To Ballance which he must pay the Master in Jersey he wanting so much of his ffraught		003:15:00
		973:05: 9½

The Conditions allowed to David Barclay and to the overseers in the Managdement of this Cargo as appeares by a resolution made by Severall of the Scotts Proprietors daited at Edenbrough the 9th ffebⁿ 1684 were; That David Barclay: should have besides his necessarie charges a lott of 10 Acres in Ambo Point, and Such provision Afterwards as is usuall in Such caises for putting off the goodes, and providing the Stock in Jersey So long as he continued with it according to the ffactorie granted him daited of May 1683, and the 3 overseers John Hanton and John Reid were to have 25th English yearlie, and for payment of the first year each a Share of ten Acres in Ambo

1 "at Abberdeen, the Ship not having roome to take." says another copy of the document. Ed.

45

Point which being accoumpted at 5ˢ a pice with 10ˢ of money they receaved in Scottland ere they went away completed theire first yeares payment the others¹ they are to have out of the Stock upon the place, and a weekes service of the Servants for each of the 4 yeares to cultivate this, the Servants according to theire Indentures are to have 25 Acres each, the trades men of them 30 paying 2ᵈ an Acre according to the generall concessions printed by all the Proprietors at London 1682 besides some particular casualties which causes some Difference according to theire capacities as the particular Indentures does witness, And it is to be noticed that this 3 lotts of 10 Acres upon Ambo point to David Barclay, John Hantone, and John Reid, as also that Sold to Bartholomew Gibson the price whereof went into this Stock is to be devided pro rato out of the Shares of all the Proprietors here concerned.—This being then a true state of the above mentioned Stock.—

Wee undersubscrivers being the persons concerned therein doe declare this to be a Just division thereof and that our respective Shares after 4 yeares when the time of the overseers and Servants doth expire which will be in or about the Month of December 1687 shall be proportioned accordingly that is all the corne and Catle and other moveable fruits and emoluments arising from the same after the crop 1687 shall be Justlie devided among us according to our interests ; but for what is immoveable to witt house, fences, and Inclosures and the Inherent Improvement of the Soile, It is to be valued by persons of known skill & Integritie appointed by the Governor and Councill for that end, and to be bought off by anie one concerned willing So to doe, paying the rest according to theire Interest, because it would make but inconvenient fractions to divide it and the dividends hardlie

46

yeald to anie one a sufficient plantation, and in caise of 2 or more concerned willing thus to purchase it, to avoide debait, the preference shall be yealded, by the votes of the Major part of the rest, it being hereby also provided, that whoever thus purchaices the improvements of the Soile Shall allow the whole number of Acres in the division of his owne Interest of 10000 Acres appointed to be sett off to each Proprietor, and to the rest nothing shall be discoumpted of theire Land for that cause, in witness of all which premises wee have Sealed and Subscrived so many copies of this Accoumpt and Instrument as may Serve all concerned, that anie one ot them being preserted to the Register of the Province may be recorded, for preservation, that an extract under his hand may Suffice to evince everie ones claime, and procure such execution for Satisfaction of all or anie one Interested as is needfull

daited in Scotland, London, and East new Jersey the fourth day of June & the   1684—

Note.—The initials " A. S.," in the first part of this document, stand for Arent Sonmans. ED.

47

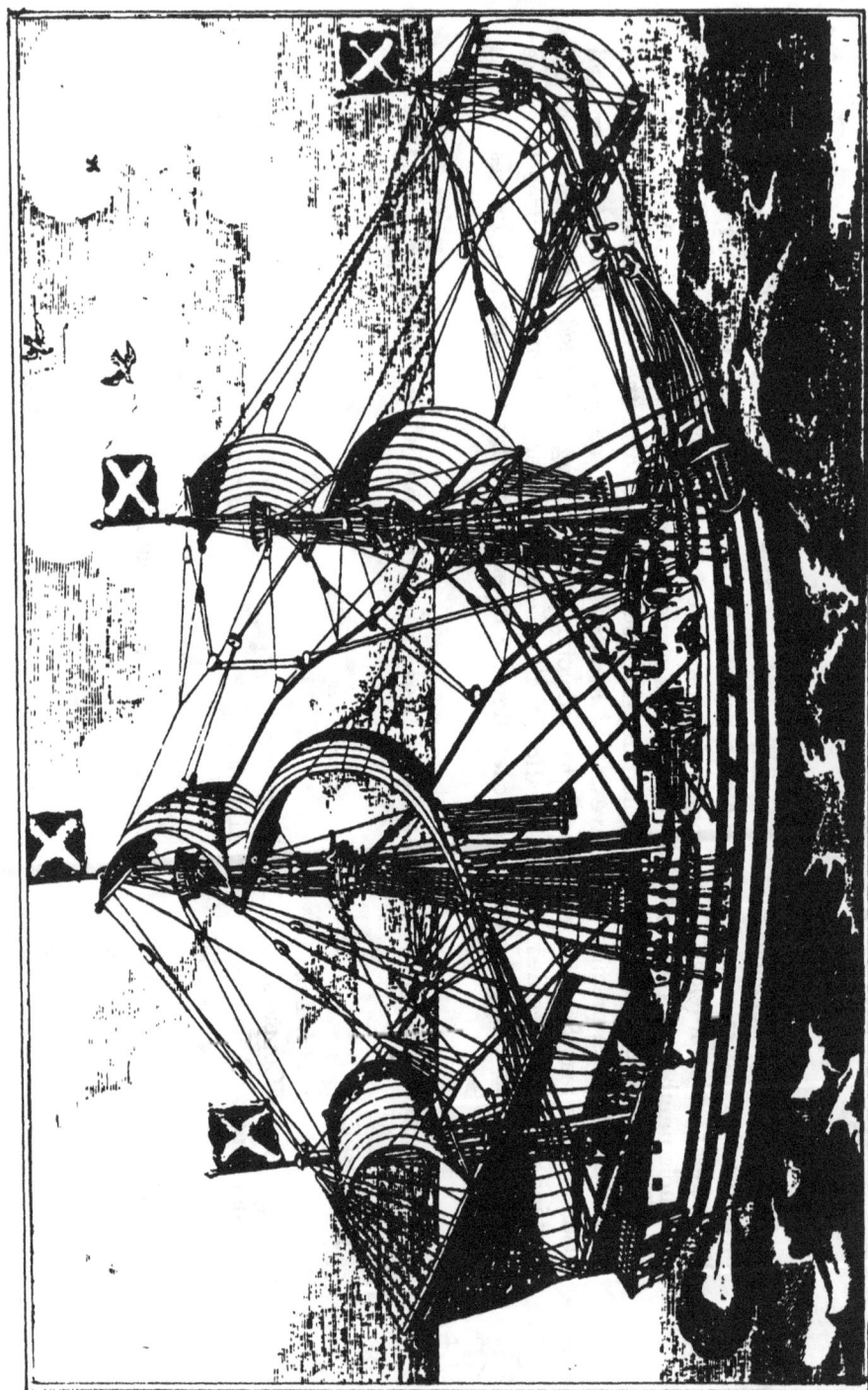

ADVERTISEMENT,

To all Trades-men, Husbandmen, Servants and others who are willing to Transport themselves unto the Province of New-Eaſt-Jerſy *in* America, *a great part of which belongs to* Scots-men, *Proprietors thereof.* [1]

WHereas ſeveral Noblemen, Gentlemen, and others, who (by undoubted Rights derived from His Majeſty, and His Royal Highneſs) are Inte-reſted and concerned in the Province of *New-East-Jersie,* lying in the midſt of the *English* Plantations in *America,* do intend (God-willing) to ſend ſeveral Ships thither, in *May, June,* and *July* enſuing, 1684, from *Leith, Montross, Aberdeen* and *Glasgow.* Theſe are to give notice to all Tradeſ-men, Huſ-bandmen and others, who are willing and deſirous to go there, and are able to Tranſport themſelves and Families thither, upon their own Coſt and Charges, to a pleaſant and profitable Countrey, where they may live in great Plenty and Pleaſure, upon far leſs Stock, and with much leſs labour and trouble then in *Scotland,* that as ſoon as they arrive there, they ſhall have conſiderable quantities of Land, ſet out Heretably to themſelves and their Heirs for ever, for which they ſhall pay nothing for the firſt four or five years, and afterwards pay only a ſmall Rent yearly to the Owners and Proprietors thereof, according as they can agree. And all Tradeſ-men, Servants, and others, ſuch as, Wrights, Coupers, Smiths, Maſons, Millers, Shoe-makers, &c. who are willing to go there, and are not able to Tranſ-port themſelves, that they ſhall be carried over free, and well maintained in Meat and Clothes the firſt four years, only for their Service, and thereafter they ſhall have conſiderable quantities of Land, ſet out to themſelves and their Heirs for ever, upon which they may live at the rate of Gentlemen all their lives, and their Children after them : Their ordinary Service will be cutting down of Wood with Axes, and other eaſie Huſband-Work, there being plenty of Oxen and Horfes for Plowing and Harrowing, &c. Let therefore all Tradef-men, Hufband-men, Servants, and others who incline to go thither, and defire further Information herein, repair themfelves to any of the Perfons underwritten, who will fully inform them anent the Countrey, and every other thing neceffary, and will anfwer and fatiffie their Scruples and Objections, and give them all other Incouragements according to their feveral abilities and capacities, viz.

At *Edinburgh* let them apply themfelves to the Lord Thefaurer-Deput, the Lord Regifter, Sir *John Gordon*, Mr. *Patrick Lyon*, Mr. *George Alexander*, Advocates, *George Drummond* of *Blair*, *John Swintoun*, *John Drummond*, *Thomas Gordon*, *David Falconer*, *Andrew Hamilton*, Merchants; at *Brunt-Island*, to *William Robison*, Doctor of Medecine; at *Montross*, to *John Gordon*, Doctor of Medecine, *John Fullerton* of *Kinaber*, and *Robert* and *Thomas Fullertons* his Brothers; in the Shire of the *Mearns*, to *Robert Barclay* of *Vrie*, and *John Barclay* his Brother; at *Aberdeen*, to *Gilbert Moleson*, *Andrew Galloway*, *John* and *Robert Sandilands*, *William Gerard*, Merchants; in the Shire of *Aberdeen*, to *Robert Gordon* of *Clunie*, and *Robert Burnet* of *Lethanty*; in the Shire of *Pearth*, to *David Toshach* of *Monyvard* and Captain *Patrick Macgreiger*; In *Merss* Shire, to *James Johnston* of *Spoteswood*; At *Kelso*, to *Charles Ormiston*, Merchant; In the *Lewes*, to *Kenith Mackenzie* younger of *Kildin*: And if any Gentleman or others be defireous to buy or purchafe any fmall fhares or portions of Land in the faid Province, they may repair to any of the forefaid Perfons, who will direct them how they fhall be ferved, providing they do it timoufly, becaufe many more Perfons are dayly offering to buy, then can be gotten well accommodated.

There is nothing more ftrange then to fee our Commons fo befotted with the love of their own mifery, that rather then quite their Native Countrey, they will live in much toyl and penury fo long as they have ftrength, being hardly able all their life to acquire fo much Riches as can fave themfelves from begging or ftarving when they grow old; mean time their Children (fo foon as they are able to walk) are expofed to the Cruelties of Fortune, and the Charity of others, naked and hungry, begging Food and Rayment

50

from thofe that either can not, or will not help them : And yet can hardly be perfwaded to go to a moft profitable, fertile and fafe Countrey, where they may have every thing that is either neceffary, profitable or pleafant for the life of Man, with very little pains and induftry; The Woods and Plains are ftored with infinite quantities of Deer and Rae, Elcks, Beaver, Hares, Cunnies, wild Swine, and Horfes, &c. and Wild-honey in great abundance : The Trees abound with feveral forts of Wine-grapes, Peaches, Apricoks, Chaftnuts, Walnuts, Plumbs, Mulberries, &c. The Sea and Rivers with Fifhes, the Banks with Oyfters, Clams, &c. Yea, the Soil is fo excellent and fertile, that the Meadows naturally produce plenty of Stra- berries, Purpy, and many more tender Plants, which will hardly grow here in Gardens : Wheat, Ry, Barley, Oats, Peafe and Beans, &c. when fown yields ordinarly 20. and fometimes 30. fold Increafe, and *Indian*-Corn, which is a Grain both wholefome and pleafant, yields ordinarly 150. and fometimes 200. fold : Sheep never mifs to have two Lambs at a time, and for the moft part three, and thefe Lambs have generally as many the next year : The Winter lafts not ordinarly above two moneths; and one Mans ordinary Labour will with eafe and plenty, maintain a Family of ten or twelve Perfons; It was no wonder then that *Ogilvie* in his New-Atlas, calls this place the Garden of the World, and the Terreftrial Paradife : Why then fhould our Countreymen, in fpite of thofe and many other Incourage- ments, be detained at home, either upon no ground at all, or upon fuch frivolous fcruples and objections as thefe are.

Firft, they alleadge that it is a long and dangerous Voyage thither! To which it is anfwered, that ordinarly it is not above 6. or 7. Weeks failing from *Scotland*, which in a good Ship, well Victualled, and with good Com- pany in the Summer time, is rather a pleafant Divertifement then a Trouble or Toyl, and it is certainly more dangerous to fail from *Leith* to *London* or *Holland*, then to *New-East-Jersy*.

Next, they fay there is no Company to be had there fave Barbarians, Woods and Wildernefs! To which it is anfwered, that this is a great miftake, for this Countrey has been Peopled and Planted thefe feveral years by gone, fo that Horfes, Oxon, Cows, Sheep, Hogs, &c. are to be fold

51

almoſt as cheap there as in *Scotland,* and ſurely they are much better being all of the *English* kinds. Nor are the Woods there any thing ſo wild and inhoſpitable as the Mountains here; Savage Beaſts there are none ſave Wolfes, and thoſe are only enemies to Sheep: The Natives are very few, and eaſily overcome, but theſe ſimple, ſerviceable Creatures, are rather an help and Incouragement, then any ways hurtful or troubleſome: and there can be no want of Company, ſeing there are many thouſands of *Scots,* *Engliſh,* and others living there already, and many more conſtantly going over, and this Summer there are ſeveral Gentlemen going from *Scotland,* ſuch as *David Toſhach* of *Monyvard,* with his Lady and Family, *James Johnston* of *Spoteswood, Kenith Mackenzie* younger of *Kildin,* Captain *Patrick Macgreiger, Robert* and *Thomas Fullertons,* Brothers German to the Laird of *Kinaber,* and *John Barclay,* Brother German to the Laird of *Vrie, William Robison,* Doctor of Medicine, and many others, who are all Perſons of good quality and Eſtates, and go not out of neceſſity, but choice.

Laſtly, they object that far fetcht Fowls have fair Feathers, and they do not believe the truth of half what is Written and Spoken in Commendation of theſe Countreys! To which it is anſwered, they may as eaſily deny the truth of every thing which they have not ſeen with their own Eyes, for all theſe things are as verily true, as that there is any ſuch pleaſant Countrey as *France, Italy, Spain,* &c. The things being matter of Fact, are Confirmed by Letters from Perſons of undoubted Credit, living on the place, and by certain Information of many Eye-witneſſes, who having once been there, can never after be induced to live in *Scotland,* nor can it be reaſonably imagined that the Perſons above-written are all Fools, to be impoſed upon by lies and Fancies; on the contrary, there are none (ſave thoſe that are wiſe in their own Eyes, but are really Ignorant) that are not undenyably convinced of the excellency of the Deſign. Let but ſuch as condemn it be ſo juſt as firſt to hear it and know it, which they may eaſily do by applying to ſome of the foreſaid Perſons, who can beſt inform them, and then if they think it not below them to be convinced, they will be forced to homologat.

VIVAT REX.

52